Halifax

ACHUSETTS

Atlantic Ocean

UT

TS

Atlantic Ocean

Bahama Is.
NEW PROVIDENCE

Gulf of Mexico

ANTIGUA

THE SAINTES

JAMAICA

Caribbean Sea

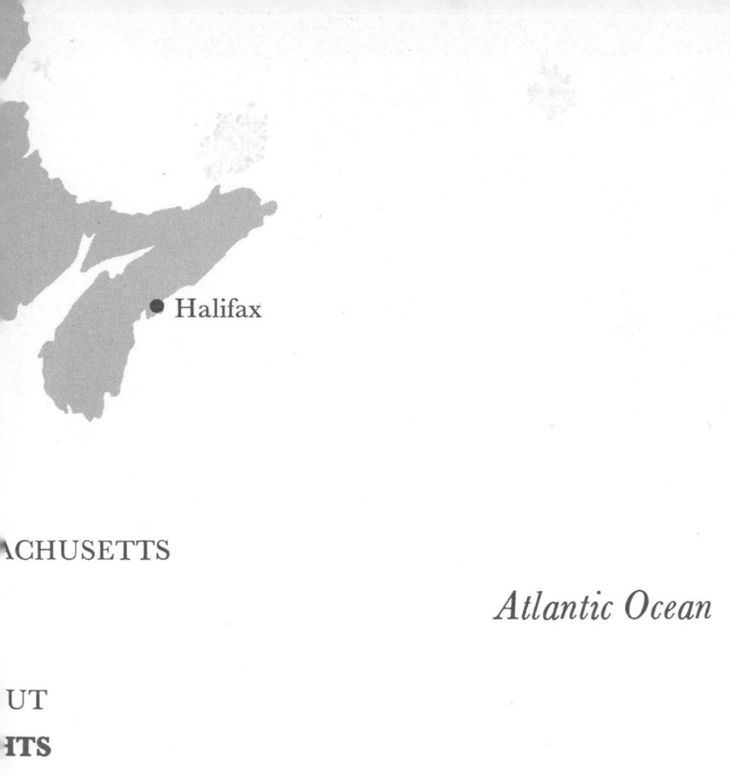

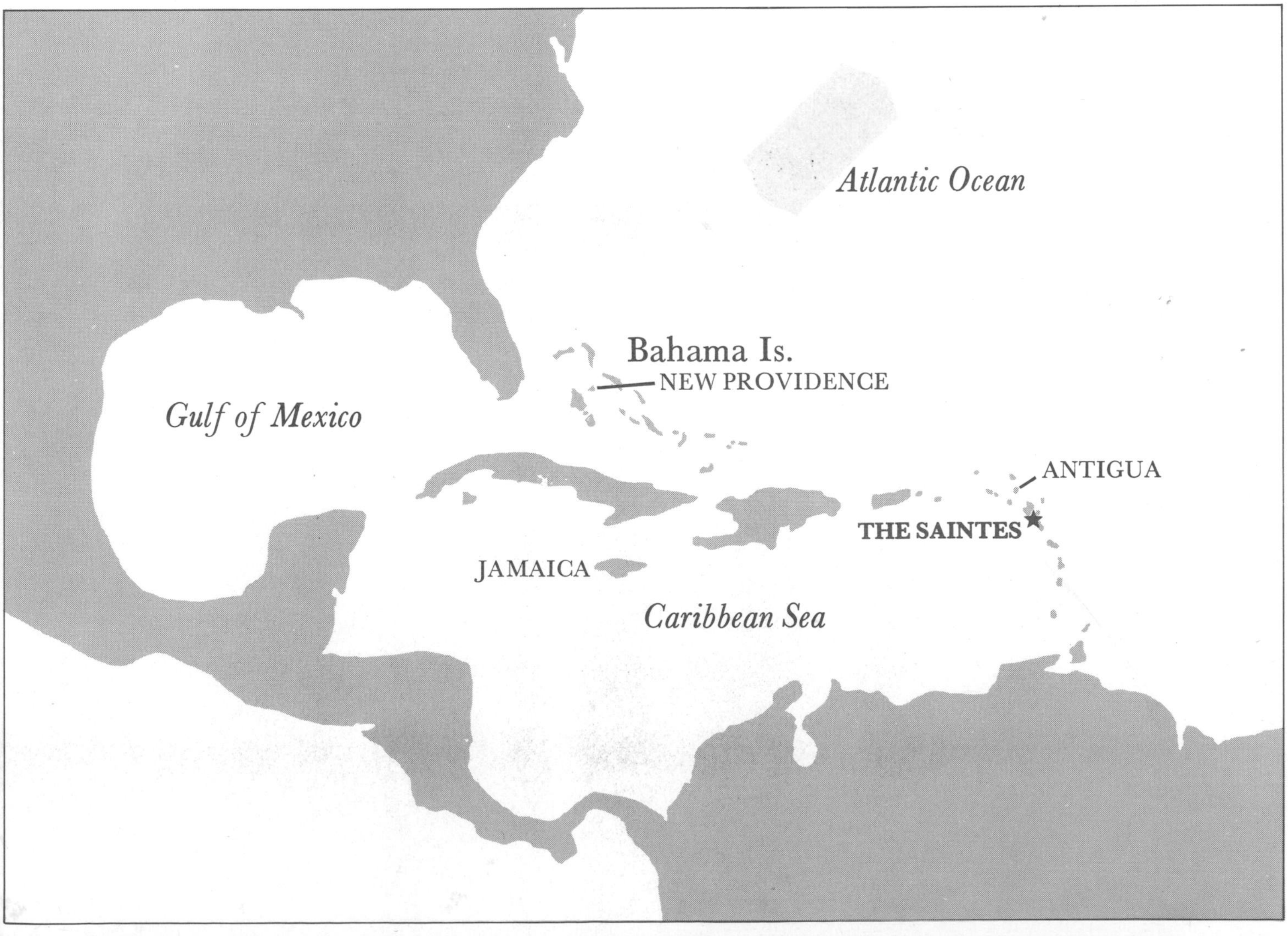

Navies of the American Revolution

Navies of the American Revolution

Antony Preston,
David Lyon and
John H. Batchelor

Prentice-Hall Inc.
Englewood Cliffs, NJ

Navies of the American Revolution
by Antony Preston, David Lyon and John Batchelor

First American Edition published by
Prentice-Hall, Inc., 1975

Printed in Scotland by
Morrison & Gibb Limited, Edinburgh

ISBN 0 13 610774 5
Library of Congress Catalog Card Number:
74-17741

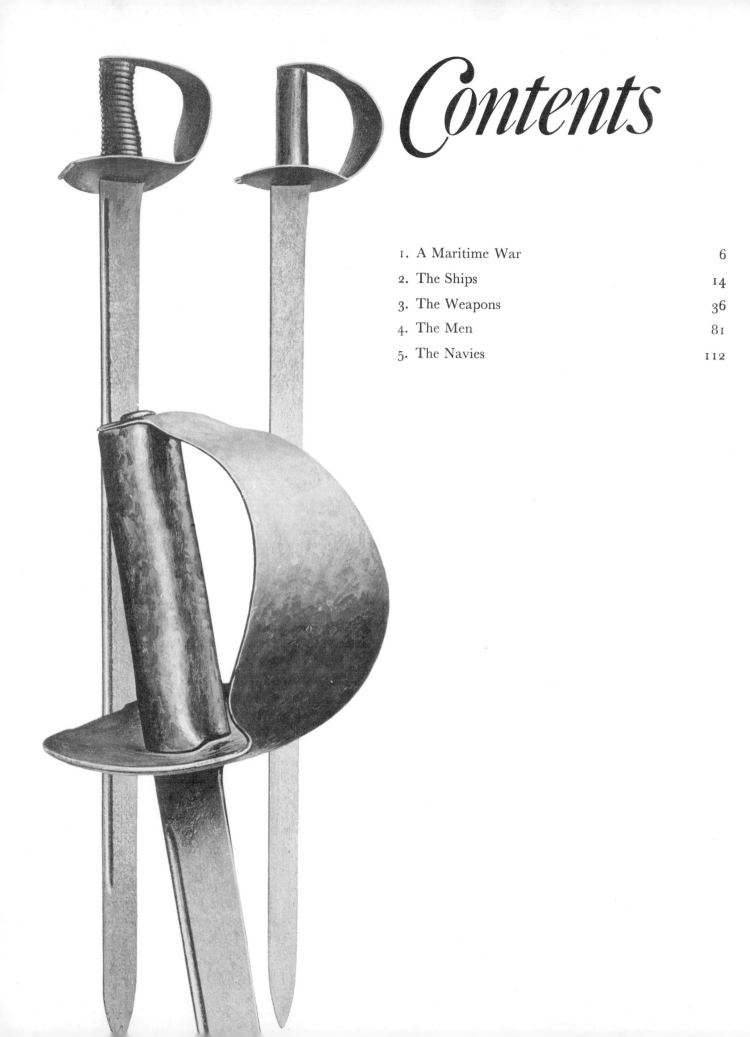

Contents

A Maritime War

The war in which America won her independence was like no other 18th century conflict. Starting as a combination of revolt and civil war in the populous colonies of the British Empire, it grew into a European war in which the British had to fight all their major rivals as well. As most of the fighting was an entire ocean away from Europe, it was a war in which navies and maritime communications played a crucial part. It was also an intensely political war, in which both Britain and her rebellious colonies were torn by faction, when no military or naval decision would be made without considering the political and diplomatic consequences.

Paradoxically, it was a struggle in which naval warfare made an absolutely vital contribution to the American victory, but in which the Americans made only a minor contribution to the naval war.

The war began, as wars will, without anyone intending it to grow so large or last so long. Britain was propelled, reluctantly and unprepared, first into police action, then into an unfamiliar and confusing mixture of guerrilla and regular warfare. A large army

Below: HMS *Royal George* (foreground) was a first-rate, 100-gun ship which sank with Rear Admiral Kempenfelt and most of her crew at Spithead in 1782.

had to be transported across the Atlantic, reinforced, provisioned and munitioned. Thus far there is a considerable resemblance to the Vietnam War, a resemblance reinforced by the covert interference of jealous rival powers, and by considerable domestic political division and opposition to the war, opposition which had its effect on the performance of the armed forces. Yet Vietnam is not a true parallel, for Britain was the mother country of the rebellious colonists, and to British commanders, the Americans were still Englishmen. Perhaps this helps to explain the reluctance of many British leaders to push operations through to a decisive conclusion.

This reluctance was reinforced by the way in which disaffection slowly slid into war; there was always the hope that the process could be stopped, that the Americans would return to their allegiance, and then everybody could go back to the time-honored task of fighting the French and Spanish. There was always the possibility of a political rather than a military solution, a possibility increased by the fact that it was an ideological war and that many Britons approved of what the Americans were doing.

Had they conducted themselves with more resolution, the British might have won the war in the first year of fighting. By the time they had agreed on a strategy for victory, they had lost their chance.

Thanks to Benedict Arnold's superb delaying tactics on Lake Champlain, the British invasion from Canada was delayed long enough for Burgoyne's surrender at Saratoga to become possible. That surrender was the signal which convinced France it was worth fighting her war of revenge. Already France had been giving undercover support and supplies to the Americans; now the next round of fighting in the great series of 18th century Franco–British naval wars began. The English Channel and its approaches became a new theatre of war, as the rival fleets sparred for advantages and tried to prevent each other sending reinforcements to the struggle across the Atlantic. The British Navy, after expanding to deal with a war of amphibious attacks and trade defense against an enemy weak at sea, had to change the tempo and emphasis of its fitting-out program to deal with a formidable rival fleet.

The French fleet had been preparing for just such an opportunity, and was strategically on the offensive. The huge British army in North America, the long lines of supply, the scattered ships of the British mercantile marine, and British colonies around the world were all vulnerable to French attack. The French with fewer merchantmen, fewer colonies, and no continental war to distract them could take their choice of targets and mount their attacks in strength. The British had to await the attacks and guard against all eventualities, and their resources of men and ships were put into a state of extreme strain which was to remain the norm until the end of the war. The only way of alleviating the strain would have been a decisive victory at sea, but that (the Battle of the Saintes) did not come until 1782, when America had already been lost.

So the French were able to send fleets to disrupt British operations in North America. They were also able to expand the war to include what became the main area of naval conflict, the West Indies. These islands were thought of at the time as sources of great wealth, more valuable even than the North American colonies, and possible bases for the exploitation of Spanish America. The West Indies were also close to the North American theatre of war, and the campaigning seasons in each area alternated. In the summer, when hurricanes made the Caribbean dangerous for ships, a fleet could be sent north. When the autumn gales began it could come back to the islands. Because of the comparative weakness of the British Navy and the pressures of the war in North America, stronger French fleets crossed the Atlantic to the West Indies than in any other 18th century war, and it was the West Indian fleets that fought more battles. In every other war the greatest part of the action was in European waters, and only in the American War did an extra-European theatre become more than a sideshow.

A year after the French declared war the Spanish joined in as well. Their main preoccupation was the recovery of Gibraltar, and so, for the rest of the war, the siege of this fortress became another element in an already complex struggle. Gibraltar remained untaken (unlike the other British Mediterranean base, Minorca), though whether its retention was worth the diversion of effort it entailed for the British fleet is a moot point. Abandoning Gibraltar early in the war might have meant that other disasters could have been averted.

In the summer of 1779 the Franco–Spanish combined fleet threatened England with invasion. The idea behind this vast armada's appearance in the English Channel was not a war of conquest. Instead the French plan was a sensible, limited, 18th century operation: the landing of troops near one or other of the two south coast naval dockyards, Portsmouth and Plymouth. The troops would occupy positions near enough to the yards for artillery to knock them into ruins. It was a good plan, and there was little the

Channel Fleet and the home defense forces could have done to prevent this catastrophe, which would effectively have knocked Britain out of the war. Fortunately for her, the plan foundered on Spain's lack of co-operation with her allies and the interminable delays which resulted, giving time for the epidemic of ship fever to catch hold. This epidemic finally caused the abandonment of the enterprise. As it was, the British had a severe fright.

The scheme of invasion was not seriously raised again. After 1779 the British fleet, with its fast copper-bottomed squadrons, could interfere with the bigger but more cumbersome allied forces that appeared in the Channel. In December 1781 British Admiral Kempenfelt showed just what could be done by swooping on a French convoy escorted by a stronger force than he had himself. The French Admiral, Guichen, had put himself on the wrong side of the convoy, and before he could react the British had captured fourteen ships. The same could have happened to an invasion convoy.

In 1782 the British eventually took advantage of the superior mobility conferred by coppering to reduce the numbers of the Channel Fleet and send the ships thus freed as reinforcements to the West Indies. It was these reinforcements that eventually secured the tardy victory at the Saintes. Had the Admiralty nerved itself to take the risk of reducing the defensive force at home earlier, the war on the other side of the Atlantic might have had a different outcome.

Meanwhile, however, the British, who for so long had managed to beat off disaster, finally failed to avert it at Yorktown. A series of British errors of judgement and mishaps, combined with the vision and daring of a French Admiral, De Grasse, led to the French having a decisive superiority at the vital point. Graves' relieving fleet failed to break through the French ships blockading Cornwallis at Yorktown. Thus a scrambling, tactically indecisive engagement off the Chesapeake was to become the greatest French victory of the war because of its strategic consequences. One of the major British armies in America was forced to surrender and it became obvious that the chance of crushing the American Revolution had gone forever. Whether this possibility of British victory in America was ever a real one will no doubt always be a subject for fierce debate. It is enough to know that Cornwallis' capitulation made it impossible. The remaining British land forces in America, still large and formidable, were restricted to holding operations, and the politicians began to look for a way out of the war without losing too much apart from America. The British naval victory over the French at the Saintes, and successful holding actions elsewhere, made a graceful British retirement from the war possible. Every other nation was also glad of the excuse to finish the war, as people were weary of the fighting. France's economy had suffered more than Britain's, with momentous consequences which became apparent with the fall of the Bastille and the beginning of the French Revolution. Spain was quite obviously not going to take Gibraltar, and Holland received no benefit out of the war, despite her efforts to stop British shipping from the North Sea to the East Indies, although the merchants of Amsterdam had hoped to recapture the American market.

Britain had lost the Thirteen Colonies, and Florida was returned to Spain, but she saved most of the rest of her empire and gained much useful experience. She had not even lost all her North American colonies. Canada remained, and also one English-speaking colony that had never rebelled, Nova Scotia, whose naval base at Halifax had been of great use to the British Navy throughout the war.

The French Navy had begun as a more effective force than ever before, and as a result came closer to beating the British than at any other time in the century. But even with Spanish and Dutch assistance, the French never quite succeeded in replacing the British as the premier naval power. The navy that did eventually achieve that a century later was born during the war, and the beginnings of the great traditions of the United States Navy give the naval side of the war an interest far greater than the comparatively small American contribution might otherwise warrant.

Two centuries after the war it is difficult to understand much that the men of 1776 took for granted. To most of us the ships of that period look bafflingly alike; to them there were clear differences of type and nationality. The task of sailing a line of battleships would be as frightening to us as the driving of a car would to them. Most of us find it hard to imagine the continuous discomfort, uncertainty and hardship of a sailorman's life. It is possibly even harder to think our way back to a world in which messages sent across the Atlantic took months, if they arrived at all. The peculiarly limited and gentlemanly nature of 18th century wars (at least for the gentlemen) is equally remote to our experience.

In this book we hope to explore at least some of the background material that will help to illuminate the how and why of the ships, guns, fleets, navies, seamen and sea battles of that momentous struggle which happened two hundred years ago.

The Ships

Construction

In the late 18th century all European and American ships were built in much the same way. Though some people were already dreaming of ships built of iron, wood was to remain the only practical material for shipbuilding for another half century. The most favored timber for the framework and covering of the hull was durable and resilient oak. Other woods were used with greater or lesser success for the hull. 'Country-built' ships made in India of teak had a good reputation, but ships built of fir in times of emergency were very short-lived. English oak was generally supposed to be the best, but even ships built of this wood had other timber in their hulls; elm was used and the decks were usually planked with fir.

A large amount of wood was needed even for the smallest ship, and the quantity required for a really large ship was prodigious. The *Royal George*, one of Britain's biggest, took 5739½ cartloads of oak, elm and

fir to build. Each cartload consisted of 50 cubic feet of timber, or the amount you might expect to get from one full-grown oak tree. It is not surprising that there was a shortage of oak, particularly of trees which had grown into the curved shapes that produced 'compass timbers'——the curved pieces necessary to make the frame of the ship. Equally important were the tall, straight pine trees from which masts were made. The timber-producing areas were strategically important, just as oilfields are now. Britain suffered from a major crisis during this war because her rebellious colonists controlled the forests of Maine, and the other mast-producing areas of Norway and the Baltic were owned by the nations which combined to form the threatening 'armed neutrality'. As a result there came a time when the 'great sticks' used for lower masts were in very short supply. The alternative was to use 'made masts', that is to say masts formed of several pieces of wood carefully slotted together. This

technique was rapidly revived in the late 1770s, but for a while British fleets, whose masts and rigging were frequently badly damaged by the successful French tactic of firing high, had to make do with hastily repaired masts and spars 'fished' together.

Shipbuilding tools were simple, most work being done by axe, two-handed saw, adze, auger and human muscle, but occasionally by sawmills driven by wind or water. Parts of the keel and parts of the stem and sternpost were fastened together by great metal bolts. These were first made of iron, but later of copper alloy, after the practice of sheathing ships' bottoms in copper had been introduced. Other joins were made with wooden pegs, where greater flexibility was needed; these pegs were variously called 'trennels', 'trunnels' or 'treenails'. A few iron nails were used, with their ends bent over after being hammered into place. The pintles, the straps and pivots on which the rudder was hung, were of iron, but, all in all, there

Far left: Figurehead from the *Royal George*.
Left: HMS *Royal George*, built in 1756. This first-rate, 100-gun ship was regarded as the finest ship of the line in the Royal Navy during the Revolutionary War period. She was a favorite flagship until she was lost at anchor in August 1782.

was less iron in a ship's hull than there was in her anchors.

The first part of a ship to be built was her keel, to which was added the stem and stern pieces. These were the biggest curved timbers in her structure, and also the hardest to find. Next came a heavy skeleton of 'ribs' or frames, which formed the basic shape of the ship, and when complete made an almost solid side, apart from the holes or 'ports' left for guns or stores. Frames were placed very close together, about one foot apart in a British line of battle ship and even closer on French ships——'the width of a cannon ball'. This was because it was very difficult to obtain lengthwise strength in a wooden structure built in this fashion, and massiveness had to compensate for lack of rigidity. Even so, 200 feet was about the practical limitation of hull length until new methods of construction were developed after the end of the century (though there were exceptions, notably the enormous Spanish *Santissima Trinidad*). Ships near the upper limit of length were particularly liable to strains caused by the movement of waves.

Once the skeleton was complete it was best to leave the hull 'in frame' to season the timber further. Normally the timber of the individual frames had already been left out in the open in great stacks for the sap to dry out, making the wood more durable. The weathering of the ship 'in frame' made doubly sure, and the *Victory* owes her extraordinary longevity to having been laid down when the previous war was ending and then being left in this state for several years before her launch. Unfortunately such a leisurely procedure was usually impossible in wartime, and many ships were built of unseasoned or green timber. They therefore became especially liable to attack by one of the deadliest enemies of wooden ships: rot, the monstrous fungoid growths that would rapidly appear in the most inaccessible parts of the hull, despite the most determined attempts at ventilation.

Some ships were planked with each plank overlapping the one below it. This method, known as 'clinker' or 'clench' building, was quite popular for small vessels, cutters and the like, but all larger ships, and the majority of the smaller ones were 'carvel' planked, with the planks laid edge-to-edge, giving a relatively smooth surface.

Planking was generally thickest underneath the ship and gradually diminished in thickness towards the topsides. Thicker bands of planking ran around the hull at intervals. These were known as 'walet', and gave the hull the lengthwise strength it would otherwise lack. The thickest and most important of these was roughly on the waterline. The frames would already be connected by beams, upon which the decks would now be laid.

The gaps between the planks of the sides and the decks were filled or 'caulked'. This caulking was never sufficient. Although the structure of a wooden ship derived advantages from its relative flexibility as the 'give' inherent in its construction made it better able to withstand the stresses of wind and weather, the disadvantage was that no wooden vessel was ever completely watertight. Very few ships could avoid the need to pump out their bilges at least once a day, while many other vessels only stayed afloat because of unremitting toil on their pumps.

After launching the ship would be towed round to her fitting-out berth by large rowing boats. Here her masts would be lowered carefully into their 'steps' situated immediately above the keel. This was done by tall 'sheer legs' which were often mounted in an old hulk. The fittings not already placed in the hull would be added, guns and stores placed on board, and the ship would be rigged and otherwise made ready for sea.

Rigging and Sailing

The rigging of a large sailing ship always looks immensely complicated to the landsman. It is in fact a beautifully calculated machine to extract power from the wind, and to support the masts. In its essentials it is, and was, extremely simple. The masts are supported by the 'standing rigging' so they can take the strain of the wind in the sails and transmit it

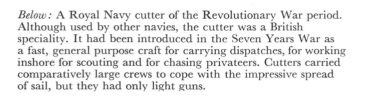

Below: A Royal Navy cutter of the Revolutionary War period. Although used by other navies, the cutter was a British speciality. It had been introduced in the Seven Years War as a fast, general purpose craft for carrying dispatches, for working inshore for scouting and for chasing privateers. Cutters carried comparatively large crews to cope with the impressive spread of sail, but they had only light guns.

to the hull. The masts are held in place fore and aft by 'forestay' and 'backstay' and are supported from the sides by the 'shrouds'. These latter serve another purpose as well, forming a ladder to enable seamen to get up the masts. Other ropes (or, as sailors always call them, lines) help to hold the masts in place, and those running fore and aft can be used to set sails on.

The 'running rigging' is used to handle the sails and the spars on which most of the sails are set. Some ropes are needed to haul spars and sails up. Others, called 'braces', pull spars (and their sails) round one

way or the other, others pull up the corners of sails for furling, and yet others hoist flags. Every rope has a purpose, and it is only the number of them that is bewildering, not their function.

The masts of a ship of any size would be composed of more than one part. The lower mast had a topmast joined or 'fidded' at its upper end. At this join would be a 'top', a platform from which the crew could operate rigging, keep a lookout and fire hand-weapons. Above the topmast might be a third part, the 'topgallant' mast. These upper masts could be

taken down at sea if necessary, though this was a tricky operation, usually done only because of bad weather or battle damage. The spars to which the sails were attached were held to the mast by heavy rope slings which gave the necessary flexibility for swinging (or 'bracing') them round to suit the direction of the wind or the maneuver intended. Sails were usually made from canvas. A ship might carry several sets, varying in thickness and area depending on whether they were intended for use in good or bad weather.

Using this basically simple machine of wood, canvas and rope, a large number of maneuvers could be, and indeed had to be, done. A sailing ship cannot sail dead into wind, though certain types of rig (which will be discussed later) and certain hull shapes can get closer to doing this than others. The nearer a ship can sail to the wind, the more 'weatherly' she is said to be; but however much she may possess this desirable quality, if her captain wants to go in the precise direction from which the wind is blowing, he has to 'tack'. This means that the ship must perform a series of zig-zags to reach her destination. Bringing a ship out of a crowded anchorage or a river needed careful control, and here the sails attached to the bowsprit would be particularly useful for swinging the head round one way or another. By carefully backing some sails while keeping others drawing, a ship could even be kept stationary with all the sails up.

The wind was not the only way to move. Intelligent

Below: The Spanish frigate *Grana*. This 30-gun ship was captured by the Royal Navy in 1781. She was very large for her armaments, reflecting the usual tendency for Spanish warships.

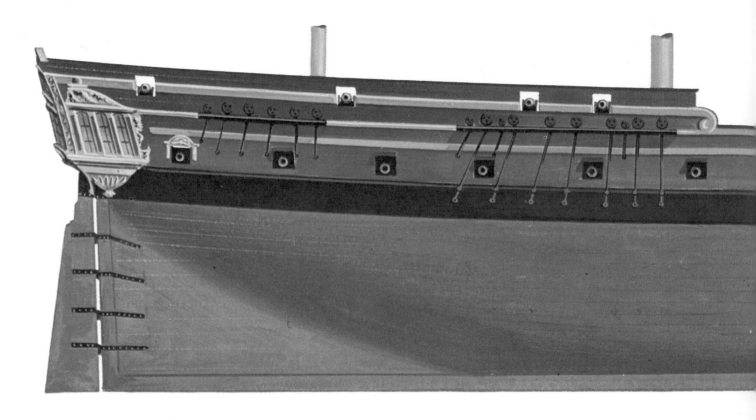

Bottom: The Dutch ship *Rotterdam*. This 50-gun ship shows the typical Dutch characteristics of stout construction and shallow draught. The Spanish joined the war in 1779 and the Dutch became allies of the French and Americans in 1781. Their entry into the war, along with the states of the Armed Neutrality, turned the Revolutionary War into a world conflict.

Below: The radeau *Thunderer*. This ungainly craft was an attempt to carry a heavy armament on a crude, easily built hull, not unlike the Thames barges of the period. Her chief disadvantage was that despite her ketch rig, she could only sail with the wind. As a result, she did not manage to get into action at the Battle of Valcour Island.

use of currents or tide could get a seaman where he wanted to go despite an adverse wind. Also ships up to the size of frigates often carried large oars called 'sweeps' which were useful in calms, while larger vessels could be dragged along by the oar-power of their boats, although towing was a slow and exhausting method of progress. Over short distances one could move by taking a line out by boat and attaching it either to an anchor, which would be dropped, or to a fixed point ashore, and then pulling in on the rope. This process was called 'warping'.

The power for all these tasks was provided by human muscle, assisted by some simple machines. Besides the blocks and pulleys used to add power to the efforts of men hauling on ropes there were windlasses and capstans. The former were used on smaller ships, the latter on larger ones and on naval vessels in general. The windlass was a sort of horizontal axle which could be turned by levers or handles and gears. The capstan was a vertical axle which could be rotated by means of bars. Both were means of obtaining extra power for the most difficult hoisting and hauling jobs, such as raising the anchor or warping the ship. The particular advantage of the capstan in a large ship was that a very large number of men could be put on to the bars. In a big ship there were usually two interconnected capstans, one immediately above the other, and situated well aft. It was impossible to get the immensely thick anchor cable around the capstan itself, so a lighter rope lashed to itself in a continuous band and passed round rollers forward would act as the 'messenger'. This was attached to the main cable by small lengths of rope called 'nippers', which were rapidly fastened to the cable as it came in through the hawse pipe, and equally rapidly detached as the cable reached the after end of the messenger. This was a task performed by the youngest and most agile members of the crew, who gradually came to be known as 'nippers' themselves. Most of the rest of the crew would be laboring around the capstans, encouraged by a fiddler sitting on top of the capstan itself. Once the anchor had been hauled out of the water it would be swung up into position by use of a block and tackle, and 'catted' to the 'cat head', in other words fastened to projections from the bow, ready to drop again if necessary.

Anchors and cables were both massive, as size was the only way of ensuring strength, and strength was essential, because a ship caught with a wind blowing it towards the land (on what was called a 'lee shore'), or in other tricky situations, would depend on the holding power of its anchor and the strength of its cable for survival. Usually several anchors of differing

sizes would be carried. At this time anchors were, as they had been for centuries, of the traditional shape, 'admiralty pattern' as it is called in England. The cross piece at the top, or 'stock' causes the spade-shaped ends of the curving piece at the bottom ('flukes') to dig into a soft bottom, or catch in something on a rocky seabed. Once this had happened the weight of the cable would play as much a part as the anchor itself in keeping the ship in position. This, of course, meant more work for the men on the capstan, and raising the anchor was always a heavy and lengthy task, even with judicious use of the sails in moving the ship to take the strain off the cable.

Hoisting out the boats from their stowage position amidships was another heavy task, done by attaching tackles to the standing rigging. The guns, as we will find out later, were also extremely heavy and awkward objects to tow. Thus it is not surprising that ships had to carry large crews, or that seamen were experts in moving heavy weights in awkward conditions by very simple means. More than one stronghold such as Crown Point was lost because seamen hoisted heavy guns up to commanding heights normally considered inaccessible.

Ship Design

Ship design has always been a compromise between several conflicting requirements. The most important of these are speed, seaworthiness, carrying capacity, strength, and maneuverability. The relative importance of each factor in the 'mix' depends on what particular task the ship is meant to do. All ships have to carry and house their crews, and the supplies to keep those crews alive. Also the 'payload' of weapons and ammunition or of cargo has to be accommodated.

At the time we are dealing with, nearly all ships were armed. Guns were very heavy objects to place in a wooden hull and were also both inaccurate, and short ranged. The more guns that could be carried the better, and the only practical way to carry large numbers of them was on the broadside. There were, as we have already seen, practical limits to the length

of a wooden ship, and both strength and stability set other limits to the number of gun decks that could be put on a hull, not to mention the bad effects of high freeboard on weatherliness. Part of the answer was to build ships with 'tumble home', with the upper decks narrower than the lower ones, and inward sloping sides above the water line. This feature had the side-benefit of making a ship harder to board, but the narrower upper deck left less room to manage sails and guns.

Heavy weights at the ends of ships caused additional strain, and made blunt bows and sterns desirable to give extra buoyancy where it was most needed. On the other hand, fine ends were desirable for speed; a box shape was obviously the best for carrying large amounts of cargo, but produced a slow and unweatherly vessel. Generally speaking, the longer a ship is the faster it can sail, but a long ship will not turn so well. In very light breezes a small ship with lots of sail up will have the advantage over a bigger one, but in bad weather the bigger ship can carry its sails for longer, and is slowed down less by the impact of waves.

For sailing ships, the ability to sail close to the wind and to turn quickly is equally important as speed, if not more so. A ship with these qualities can still get away from a fundamentally faster vessel without them. However big and heavily armed a ship is, she is of little value if she cannot sail well enough to move from place to place as needed, or if she is so built to be unable to stand up to the strains of a storm at sea.

Specialist requirements, such as shallow draught, also affect the whole compromise of design. Shallow draught entails a lessening in the ability of a ship to sail to windward, though this handicap can be reduced by using hinged 'lee boards' on the sides which can be lowered to make a sort of temporary keel. An even more efficient solution is the centreboard, and one British officer who fought on Lake Champlain during this war, Schanck by name, was already working on this idea. Another specialist requirement for bomb vessels, the heavy construction

necessary to take the recoil of their mortars, made them heavy craft to sail.

No one ship could be totally satisfactory in all directions, so there was in our period, as later, specialization of types. The larger warships concentrated on size, strength and gun-carrying, the smaller ones on weatherliness and speed, the middle-sized ships, the frigates, were about the nearest to an all-round compromise.

With merchantmen the choice of qualities depended mainly on the particular trade. East Indiamen concentrated on size and defensive strength; ships of the coastal trade could carry big cargoes, but were also both weatherly and maneuverable (as Captain Cook knew when he chose ships of this type for his explorations). Ships built in the American colonies, often involved in smuggling or sailing in dangerous waters, tended to be particularly fast and weatherly.

The French had always built comparatively large ships in each class. They had the reputation of being the best ship designers, and they were the first to introduce the new standard types which became the main equipment of the navies of the second half of the century: the 74s, 64s and frigates. The Spanish were quick in following suit, and they too tended to build large ships for their rate. Unlike the French, who tended to build for speed, the Spanish preferred to build heavy ships which were particularly high out of the water. In contrast, the British usually produced smaller ships, and provided them with more guns, but with lines which were not as fine as those of the French. This comparative smallness was, strictly speaking, not a design matter at all, but would come under what is nowadays called the 'staff requirement', a matter for the policy-makers rather than the designers.

The Americans, once they started to build warships, were noted for long and narrow ships, big for

Left: A section through a horse transport. Troopships and transports were the main means of supplying the British Army and Navy throughout the Revolutionary War. Normally they were ex-merchant ships and often underwent alterations to enable them to handle their military cargoes. Special slings were provided to minimize the injuries and distress that horses always suffered on a sea passage.
Below: The first recognition of the Stars and Stripes by a foreign government, when the USS *Ranger*, commanded by John Paul Jones, was saluted by French warships at Quiberon Bay.

their class, and remarkable for their speed. They showed the promise, later fulfilled, of taking over from the French the leading place in frigate design. On the other hand American ships were not noted for their durability. As a contemporary naval architect put it, of the American prizes considered suitable for war 'not one tenth part were considered worthy of employ when in the hands of their captors'.

The other contestants in the war——the Dutch, Swedes, Danes and Russians——all favored shallow-draught, flat-bottomed ships that were good for operations close inshore, but tended to be unstable in heavy weather.

Rigs and ship types

There were many different types of vessel at this time, often differing greatly in appearance, but there is, alas, no great degree of standardization in the words used to describe these different types. The same word might be used to describe several types of rig, or the way a ship was built, or its function; while several different words might be used to describe what was essentially the same type of vessel. It was not until nearly a century later that words such as 'bark' (or barque) and 'sloop' came to mean only a particular sort of rig, rather than a hull type or function. By the time of the American Revolution the word 'frigate' was settling down to its generally accepted meaning of a particular type of medium-sized warship, but it can still be found in some documents of the late 18th century in its earlier meaning of any small fast ship. The whole confused situation is splendidly summed up in a definition taken from a nautical dictionary of 1750 (Blankney's *Naval Expositor*): 'Sloops are sailed and masted as Mens' Fancies lead them, sometimes with one mast, with two and with three, with Bermudoes, Shoulder of Mutton, Lugg and Smack sails; they are in figure either square or round and stern'd.'

Bearing all this in mind it is still possible to distinguish the main types of vessel. All the larger warships and merchant ships were three-masted vessels with square sails on all three masts, confusingly known simply as 'ship rig'. Although basically square rigged, most 'ships' by this time carried a full outfit of fore and aft sails as well: jibs and other headsails between foremast and bowsprit, staysails between the masts, and the 'spanker' on the mizzen (aftermost) mast. This last sail had replaced the older lateen (triangular) sail, though the long yard projecting forward of the mizzen mast still remained in the bigger warships till nearly the end of the century, as a useful reserve if a mast needed replacing.

'Ketch' rig had been a popular one for smaller ships earlier in the century but was now going out of favor. It was basically that of a 'ship' with the foremast removed. In other words there was a tall mainmast and a smaller mizzen. By the middle of the century a new two-masted rig was coming into general favor, both for merchantmen and warships. The 'Brig' had two square rigged masts of approximately equal height and required fewer men to handle than a 'ship', while retaining most of the advantages of that rig. Also round the 1750s two other rigs were adopted for naval use in smaller warships. The single-masted 'Cutter' was particularly popular in the British Navy. The two masted fore-and-aft rigged 'Schooner' had been developed in American waters from a much smaller European type and was a most weatherly rig.

If cutters and schooners can be considered to be British and American specialties in small fast vessels, the French equivalent would be the 'Lugger', and that of Spain and the Barbary States was the 'xebeck'. Both featured various combinations of square and lateen sails. The modification of ship rig in which the mizzen mast only carries fore and aft sails, later to be known as the 'barque' was comparatively rare at this time, being largely confined——like the 'xebeck'—— to the Mediterranean. There were many other varieties of rig for small local coasting craft, but we need not consider them here.

Warships of this period were divided into two main groups. Any (shiprigged) ship of 20 guns or above was 'rated'. There were six Rates, divided according to the

number of guns carried. The 'first rates' (100 guns or over) and the 'second rates' (98 to 90 guns) were the flagships, the 'super-heavies', few in number, but very powerful, with three complete decks of guns. The standard fighting ships of the day were the 'third rates' (between 64 and 84 guns). Nearly all third rates were two-deckers (i.e. two complete gun decks.) First, second and third rate ships were known as 'line of battle ships' or 'ships of the line'. These were the ships fit to lie in the main fighting formation of the day, the 'line of battle'. Anything below a 64-gun ship was considered too lightly armed and weakly built to be included in the line, though exceptions were made.

The smaller two-deckers do not easily fit into the rating system. They were no longer considered fit to lie in the line, but were placed there in emergencies or used as escorts for convoys, as flagships on distant stations, and so on. These ships might be fourth rates (50 to 60 guns) or even the larger fifth rates (30 to 44 guns). In some ways they were analogous to the heavy cruisers of World War II.

The frigates, included in the middle and lower ranges of the fifth rates, were very much in favor. They were ships of between 28 and 40 guns, with a single gun deck, plus quarter deck and forecastle. They were the most glamorous warships of the time, fast and comparatively powerful, a sort of combination of cruiser and destroyer. The larger ones were fifth rates, the smaller ones in the sixth rate (20 to 28 guns).

The smaller sixth rates, the 24s and 20s, though sometimes called frigates, strictly speaking were too small for this title. In the British Navy they were usually known as 'Post Ships'. They were the smallest ships to be commanded by an officer of the rank of

Captain. In the French Navy the term 'corvette' was used to describe them.

Next below the rated ships were 'sloops', a loosely defined class of vessel carrying between eight and twenty guns, the rig being either ship or brig, though there were also cutters and schooners classed as sloops at this period. However, vessels of these latter rigs were more often classed by themselves. The 'unrated' classes included a large number of other types, bombs, fireships, armed ships, transports, etc.

It should be emphasized that the number of guns given for ships under this 'rating' system was an official number which might not correspond to the actual number carried. Frequently a Captain might manage to squeeze another couple of guns aboard; more rarely, he might take a few out of the ship to lighten her. Equally, a ship might be 'pierced' for more guns that she actually carried, that is, she might have more gunports than guns. The number of guns carried was always supposed to be that of 'carriage guns', in other words of guns mounted on the usual 'truck carriage' of the day. The small 'swivel' guns and hand weapons were not counted. This was reasonable enough, until the carronade began to come into service late in the war. This was a cannon mounted on a slide and was not considered as a carriage gun, though it was at least as powerful. Thus a ship carrying a large number of carronades would be listed as only having a small armament, when in fact it had a much bigger one. Confusion compounded!

When a warship of any kind was sent off on an independent mission by itself, it was referred to as a 'cruiser', a word which did not mean a specific type of ship, as it does now. Ships which were laid up in

Left: Fire ships were not just old ships which were ready for the scrapheap. Modifications were made to them which enabled fire to do the most damage to anything these ships touched. The gunports were altered to drop *down* when retaining ropes burned through inside the ship; this allowed flames to shoot out through the sides of the fireship to the target. Simple rockets were also set to fire at angles aimed to set rigging and sails alight.

Below: A frigate of the Royal Navy. The frigate was the 'maid of all work' of the Fleet, and was the favored command of ambitious young officers. She was capable of outstanding any heavier warship, and her main duties were scouting for the main fleet, the protection of one's own commerce, and the destruction of the enemy's shipping. In most cases a frigate could only be brought to action by one of her own kind, and so many of the classic single-ship actions of the period were between frigates.

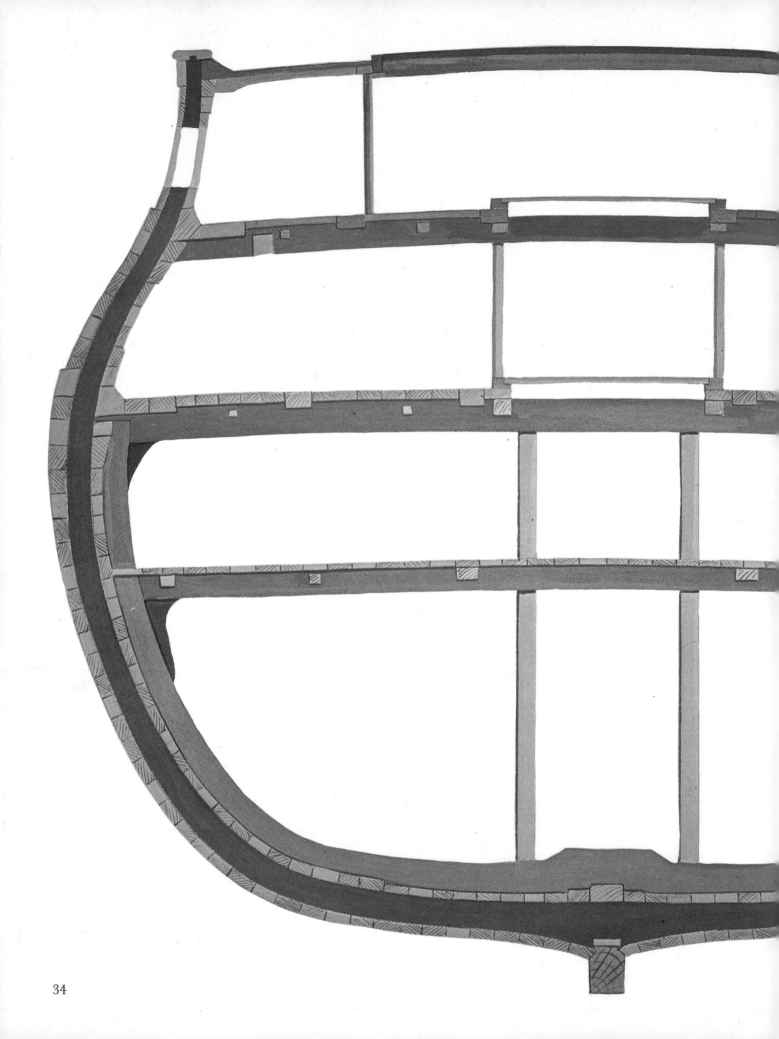

34

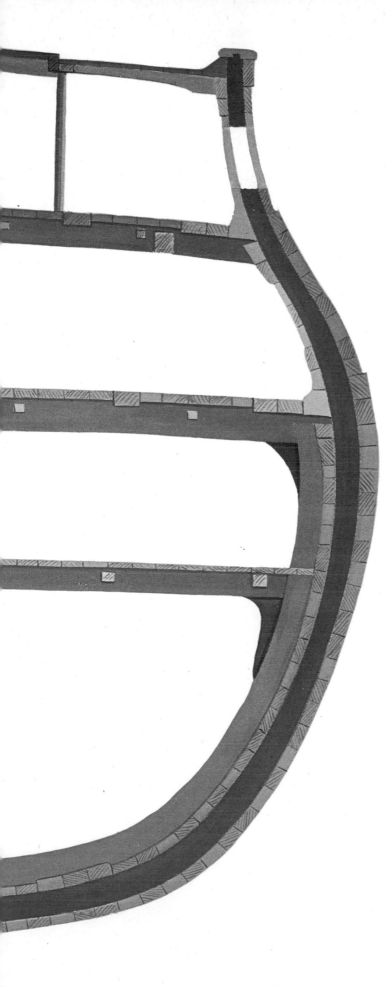

Left: A section through a typical French frigate showing its construction. The French built the first true frigates, but the type was soon copied by the British and others.

reserve were said to be 'in Ordinary': in this state the masts had been taken out, and often a roof was built over the hull to keep out the weather. Some ships not actually in full use might be fitted out as 'guardships' with masts and guns back on board, partly stored and given a skeleton crew. It was comparatively easy to complete the fitting out of a ship in this state. Larger warships were sometimes employed as transports, with their lower deck guns taken out to create more room, and with only their upper deck guns left. The empty gun ports looked like the holes in a flute, so a ship in this state was said to be '*en flûte*'.

Merchant ship types were usually named after their trades: 'East Indiaman', 'West Indiaman' or 'Collier Bark', though the smaller ships had more general names such as 'hoy', 'bilander', 'felucca' etc. 'Privateers' were neither naval nor mercantile. They were private-enterprise warships, owned and equipped by private citizens who purchased a privateering commission or 'Letter of Marque', and could then fit out an armed vessel to capture enemy ships for profit. Any sort of ship could be used; indeed the French often used open boats with no guns, but full of armed men, which were quite capable of taking a lightly armed merchantman. The Americans did much the same with large whaleboats. Usually a privateer was a ship chosen for the speed necessary to catch merchantmen and avoid warships, with a big crew for boarding and for manning prizes, and a reasonable gun armament. Privateers tried to avoid action with a warship because of the danger and the lack of profit, but there were several cases of large American privateers taking British warships. Brigs and schooners were most favored as privateers, but the British captured at least one 64-gun French privateer, and the Spanish also produced some very large privateers.

This peculiar method of waging war for profit was practiced by all nations. The British, with the largest merchant fleet, were the main sufferers, but it did not stop the merchants of London, Bristol and Liverpool fitting out their own privateers with as much zest as their rivals in Boston, Philadelphia or St. Malo.

The Weapons

The battle-winning weapons of the American War were smooth-bore cannon or 'carriage guns' mounted on 'truck carriages', the standard naval gun mounting of the day. 'Trucks' were the small solid wheels on which the gun moved. They were basically very simple weapons, the cannon barrel being merely a long iron tube closed at one end, and increasing in thickness towards the back to gain more strength in the area where firing produced the greatest strain. On either side of this barrel just forward of the centre

of balance, were cylindrical protrusions on which the gun rested when in its carriage. These were called 'trunnions'. Some older guns might still have a pair of handles on their upper side, called 'dolphins', often being ornamented like that beast; they were useful in handling the barrel, but were going out of fashion by the end of the 18th century.

The techniques of iron founding had been improved to the point when guns made of that metal were stronger than bronze ones, as well as being less liable to deform after heavy use. Above all, iron guns were considerably cheaper. The main advantage of bronze guns was that you could melt them down and use them again, an advantage which also applied to the comparatively new use of brass for weapons. Pictures drawn in the newly built brass foundry at Woolwich Arsenal just before the war show French guns captured in the previous war being melted down to make new mortars and howitzers. Old iron guns were only good for ballast.

Below: The *Buckingham* ready for launch. A third-rate, 70-gun ship, she was launched in 1751 and is typical of the majority of ships of the line of the British fleet during the Revolutionary period. The *Buckingham* became the store ship *Grampus* during the war and was lost at sea in 1778.

Below: A section through a cannon showing the sequence of loading cartridge, wad and ball, and wad with cartridge pricker down the touchhole, which pierced the cartridge paper, insuring that the priming powder ignited the main charge.
Bottom left: An English cannon on its carriage.
Bottom right: A section through a typical British ship of the line, showing how her three gundecks were constructed. The 'tumblehome' made the upper decks narrower to reduce topweight without sacrificing height above the water line.

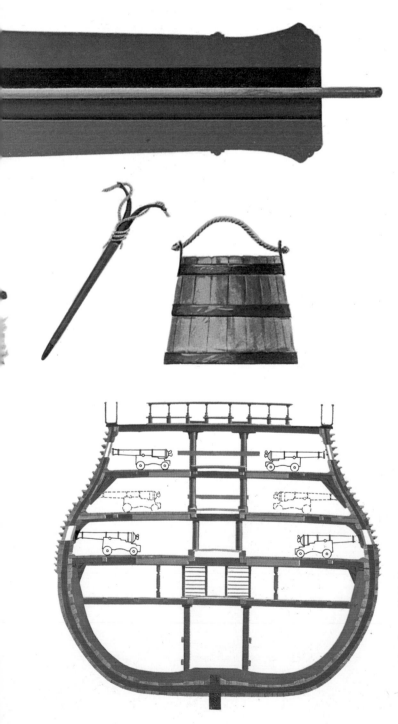

A gun was operated by using a system of ropes and pulleys to run it up, or to train it from side to side ('traversing'). This latter operation was assisted by the use of 'hand spikes' to lever the carriage round. The barrel was raised ('elevated') or lowered ('depressed') by the use of wedges. The gun would be loaded when it was 'inboard'——i.e. run back towards the centre of the ship. If the gun had been fired recently it would be sponged out, to remove any burning fragments of the powder cartridge left in the barrel, a very necessary precaution to prevent a premature explosion as the gun was being loaded. A bag 'cartridge' of gunpowder would then be pushed to the back of the barrel, followed by a wad of felt, then the shot, then, usually, another wad to hold the cannon ball in place. All was rammed home, then a spike would be pushed through the 'touch hole' at the breech of the gun, to make a hole in the cartridge, and a little fine gunpowder added to carry the flame through to the cartridge. The gun would then be 'run out' so that the muzzle pointed out of the port, and the aim was adjusted. The cannon was fired by the glowing end of a slow-match being applied to the gunpowder in the touch hole. The recoil of the gun would be taken up partly by its own weight, partly by the rolling resistance of the trucks and the upwards slope of the deck towards the centre line, and finally by thick rope 'breechings' which prevented the gun rolling back too far. After a while the force of repeated explosions would widen the touch hole, until far too much of the hot gases blew back up this hole. It would then be 'bushed'——an iron plug inserted and a new touch hole drilled through it.

Obviously the operation of a gun of any size required a lot of manpower, particularly if one bears in mind that when the racks of ready-use shot beside the guns had been emptied, new cannon balls had to be fetched up from below, along with more cartridges. The full crew of what was to become the largest British naval gun, a 32-pounder, numbered fifteen (though a smaller number could fire the gun in emergencies). This team had to be drilled in per-

Below: Working the guns. Positions of the gun crew before loading (*left*), loading (*centre*), and training the gun (*right*). Number 1 was the gun captain, 2 the second captain, 3 the loader, 4 the sponger, 5 assistant loader, 6 assistant sponger. The rest of the crew were auxiliary members of the team who manned the side and training tackles. When loading number 3 (the loader) placed the cartridge, wad and ball into the barrel, while number 4 (the sponger) rammed home each of these in turn. Because of their exposed positions, they were more likely to get injured by splinters or direct hits than anyone in the crew. If this were to happen, numbers 5 and 6 took over their positions.

Bottom: A French cannon on its carriage.

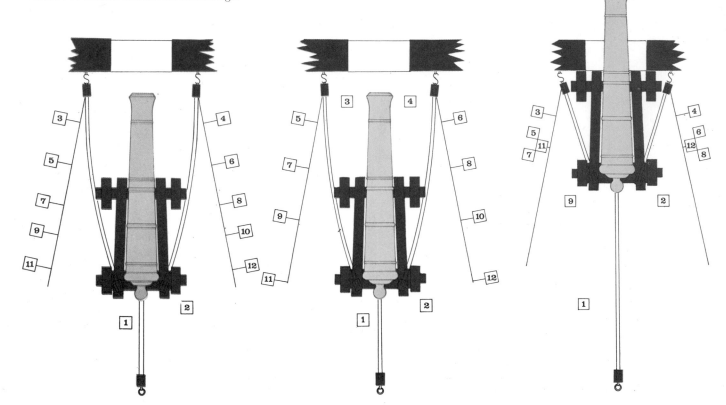

forming the complex series of operations of loading and firing their weapon until they could do this in correct sequence and with the greatest possible speed amid the choking and blinding smoke, cramped conditions, shattering noise and ever-present danger of a naval battle.

To be effective, fire had to be both rapid and accurate. Rapidity was obtained by constant practice and intelligent organization; accuracy was more difficult to obtain. Manufacturing tolerances were large, and a relatively large 'windage', the gap between the cannon ball and the inside of the barrel, had to be allowed for. Matters had been improving with the successive developments in iron working techniques and the new method of casting a gun solid, then boring it out, was clearly better than the old way of casting the barrel hollow.

Maximum 'random' range could be as much as two miles, but there was little chance of hitting at that range. A skilled gunner with a good gun, specially chosen ammunition, firing with care in ideal conditions, might perhaps get a hit at a mile or more. The effective range of average guns and gunners was nearer a quarter of a mile, but 'pistol shot' or, better still, 'Biscuit's toss' or 'yardarm to yardarm' were preferred in battle. At close range, concentrating on rate of fire rather than accuracy, a good gun crew could fire off perhaps 7–8 shots in five minutes. The ideal was to fire all the guns in one great simultaneous broadside for maximum moral effect, but even the best-trained ships could not keep this up for any length of time, since the slower gun-crews and those which had suffered casualties would fall behind the rest. Often, instead of the full broadside, 'ripple firing' was used, with each gun fired in quick succession after its neighbor, to reduce the strain on the fabric of the ship.

Usually the gun captain would wait until the roll brought his sights onto target before firing. Firing on the down-roll was done when the aim was to 'hull' an enemy, hitting him, with luck, on the waterline, while firing on the up-roll was the correct way of trying to damage his masts and rigging. The British favored the former, the French the latter.

At short range individual guns could achieve a 'shotgun' effect by firing many small projectiles instead of one large one. This took various forms. 'Grapeshot' was a bundle of small cannon balls, 'canister' or 'case shot' was a tin or cardboard container of bullets or small shot which would burst and spread out after leaving the muzzle. Scraps of old iron, nails and the like in a bag would produce much the same effect. This was called 'langridge', and was used by privateers and merchantmen rather than by navies. When the main aim was to damage an enemy's rigging and masts, various kinds of 'dismantling shot' could be used to give a greater chance of hitting. The oldest forms were 'bar shot' and 'chain shot'. In the former two iron balls, or halves of balls, were connected by a bar. This dumb-bell shaped projectile would swing through the air to cut ropes and shatter spars. Chain shot was a similar type of projectile, with two balls connected by a length of chain. The French experimented a good deal with other kinds of dismantling shot. One type which emerged was a ball with bars attached to it on a ring. When the shot left the gun the bars would swing out and endanger anything in their way.

All these projectiles had the disadvantage that they were very inaccurate and short-ranged. Long-range firing could only be done by using a solid ball of iron, usually called a 'shot, the traditional cannon ball, used to smash an opponent's hull. A 32-pounder ball fired at a muzzle velocity of some 1600 feet per second could penetrate about $2\frac{1}{2}$ feet of oak planking. If shots hit the thinner planking of the topsides they would produce a shower of deadly splinters, and might well dismount a cannon or smash its carriage, as well as dismembering anyone unlucky enough to be in its path. Sometimes, when fire was opened at close range, guns would be 'double shotted', loaded with two balls, to give an even more devastating effect.

If a captain could place his ship across the bow or

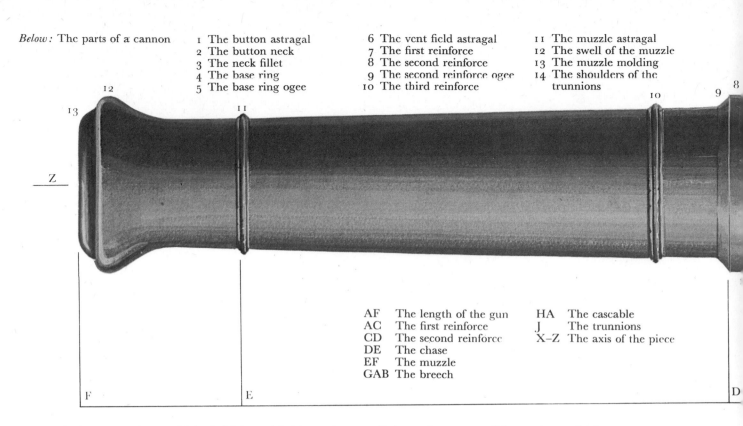

Below : The parts of a cannon

1 The button astragal	6 The vent field astragal	11 The muzzle astragal
2 The button neck	7 The first reinforce	12 The swell of the muzzle
3 The neck fillet	8 The second reinforce	13 The muzzle molding
4 The base ring	9 The second reinforce ogee	14 The shoulders of the
5 The base ring ogee	10 The third reinforce	trunnions

AF	The length of the gun	HA	The cascable
AC	The first reinforce	J	The trunnions
CD	The second reinforce	X–Z	The axis of the piece
DE	The chase		
EF	The muzzle		
GAB	The breech		

stern of his enemy, he could 'rake' him with his entire broadside, while the enemy captain could at best reply with the few guns mounted to fire ahead or astern. In addition, the bow and the stern, were the weakest parts of the ship. Instead of having to penetrate the thick timbers of the side, shots fired at the bow or stern could pass through the length of the ship, leaving a trail of destruction behind.

When a shore battery was firing on a ship and the danger of setting fire to oneself did not exist, the gun could fire shot which had been heated in a furnace till it was glowing red. Even so this was a very dangerous and skilled business for the gunners, who had to handle their projectiles with extreme care, and use very thick, wet wads to prevent the heat of the shot setting off the gun while it was being loaded. When a red hot shot hit a ship and buried itself in its timbers, unless rapidly and heavily doused in water, fire would soon break out. Once that had happened, the ship was probably doomed.

Naval cannon were all very similar in their appearance, the biggest being only scaled-up versions of their smaller cousins. The proportions of both gun and carriage varied very little, only the size changed. Cannon were classified, as has probably already become obvious, by the weight of shot fired. The biggest cannon, British 42-pounders and French 46-pounders, were already dropping out of favor because they were so heavy and cumbersome, and for this reason, very slow firing. It was better to have

a lighter, less powerful weapon which was more use at sea. In the British battleship this meant the 32-pounder; in the French, 36. Most navies had standard types roughly similar to the British cannon which ran in sequence from 42- and 32-pounders, through 24-, 18-, 12-, 9- and 6-pounders, and then on down to the small 4- and 3-pounders.

Mortars. Explosive shells were never fired from cannon at sea. Shells fired from ships required a special weapon, the mortar, and were used purely for shore bombardment. A French invention dating from 1682, naval mortars were carried on specially designed ships called bomb vessels. Mortars looked like great cooking pots with immensely thick walls. Their trunnions were at the back, and they rested on a bed, for they fired their projectiles up into the air so that they fell on the target from a height. Firing mortars was an altogether more scientific form of gunnery, and could be done accurately from a great range.

A shell was a hollow ball, with a hole at the top through which it was filled with gunpowder, and into which a wooden plug was then screwed. There might be a raised lip round the hole, and some shells were given raised lugs on the upper surface to make them easier to carry. The wooden plug in the hole had a fuse running through it, which could be cut short at any one of several points to give different burning times for that fuse. With practice a shell could be made to burst just before it hit the target, and this airburst effect would scatter lethal fragments of the

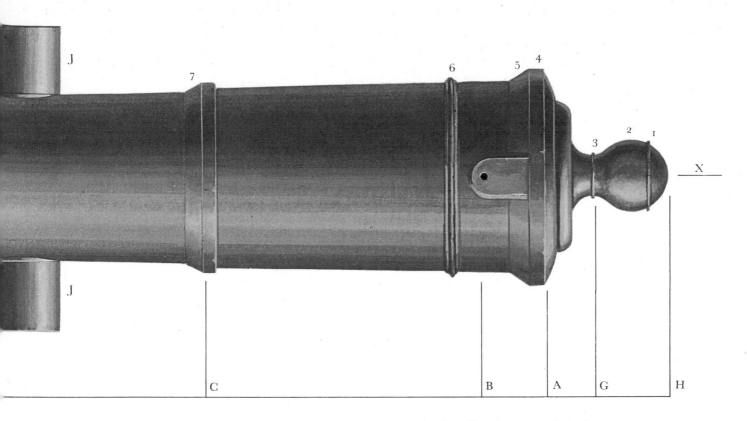

casing over a wide area. On the other hand, it was also possible to delay the explosion until the shell had penetrated buildings or dugouts. At first, lighting the fuse was something of a problem because if the fuse was alight and the mortar then failed to fire, lethal difficulties would arise. The problem was finally solved by relying on the flash of firing the mortar to set the fuse alight, a satisfactorily simple method.

The number of shots a bomb vessel could fire were limited. In his great and successful bombardment of the French invasion fleet at Le Havre during the Seven Years War, Rodney kept his bombs firing for a whole day. By the end of it not only had the British used up nearly all their ammunition, not one mortar was fit to fire, and most were cracked or burst. So great was the strain of prolonged firing that all bomb vessels were making water fast, and some were nearly falling to pieces.

The larger bomb vessels were usually ketchs, the absence of the foremast providing the mortars with a comparatively free field of fire. Bomb vessels carried two mortars each, of about 10- or 13-inch calibre. Little 'coehorn' mortars, the baby brothers of these monsters, were made for use on boats, tops or by

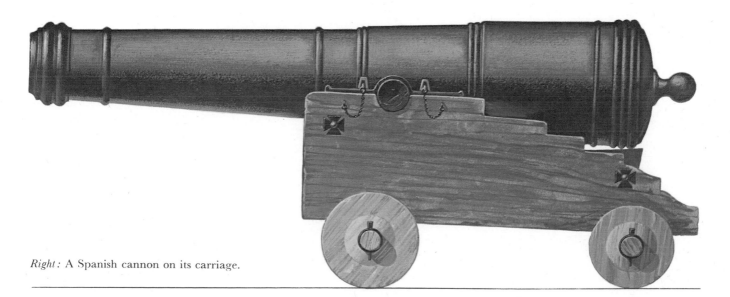

Right: A Spanish cannon on its carriage.

Below: A bomb vessel showing the heavy construction to withstand the massive recoil of the mortar. Note the method of stowage of the bombs.
Opposite bottom: A mortar.
Opposite top: Iron swivel guns.

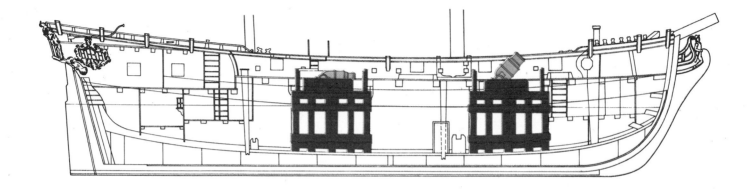

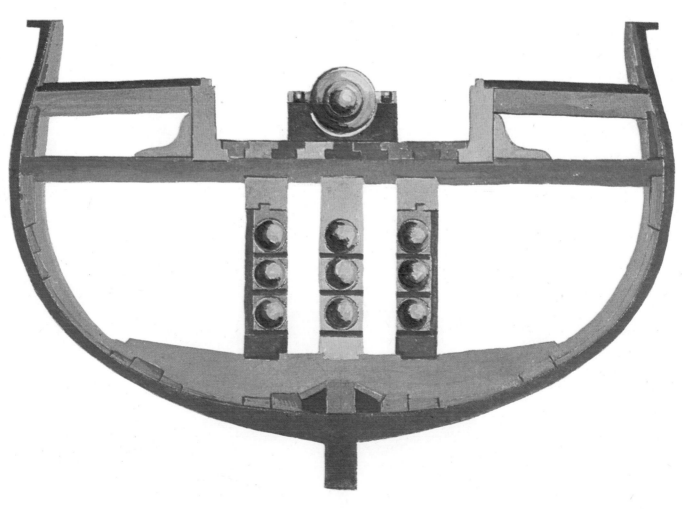

landing parties. Howitzers, a sort of compromise between cannon and mortar, were much used ashore but rarely found on board ship, though there are records of them having been used by the British Lake Champlain Flotilla in the radeau *Thunderer*, probably because they were readily available from the army.

Small Arms

Most ships carried weapons which were half way between cannons and muskets. These were the 'swivels', man-killing firearms which took a half-pound shot. They were too heavy to fire unsupported, and so were mounted in forked supports placed on the top of wooden uprights on the 'gunwales' (it can be seen from this how the name arose). Swivels could also be carried up to the 'fighting tops', the platforms half way up the mast, from which a deadly fire could be directed at the enemy's decks. Some swivels had a sort of pistol grip, or a 'rat tail' attached to the back to point them with. Others might have a stock, like over-sized muskets. Some small merchantmen were armed

with nothing but swivels, and these weapons formed a substantial part of the armament of most cutters, and other small vessels. They were particularly useful in repelling boarding parties or nearby boats.

As we have seen, most battles were fought at close range, close enough for small arms to be of major importance, while the hand-to-hand fighting by boarding parties was the approved way to end most battles. The usual firearm used before the boarding started were muskets, supplemented by blunderbusses and, especially in American ships, rifles. 'Sea Service' muskets and rifles were little different from the weapons used ashore (described in more detail in the companion to this volume *Armies of the American Revolution*). Blunderbusses, which were bell-mouthed, wide bore firearms, loaded with several slugs, or a collection of bits of iron, were lethal weapons at close range against boarders. They were particularly popular on merchant ships.

Hand-to-hand fighting was done with boarding pikes, cutlasses, pistols, clubbed muskets, tomahawks,

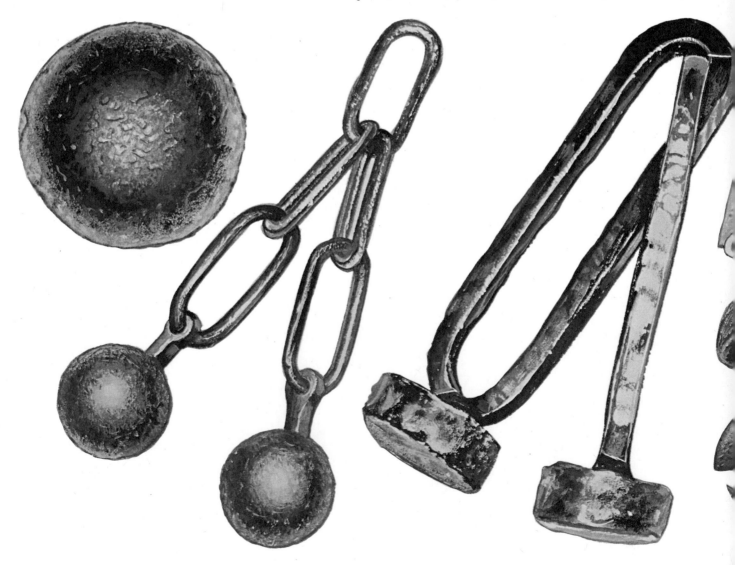

knives and anything else that came to hand. The boarding pike was a wooden pole about six feet long with a narrow steel point on the end. It was a particularly nasty and effective weapon in defense, useful for prodding boarders who were trying to clamber over the nets usually rigged on going to action stations.

Fighting on the cramped decks of a sailing ship was a close-in business. There was little room for swinging long weapons, or indulging in brilliant swordplay, and the swords used were therefore short, usually curved, relying more on the edge than the point. The cutlass used by seamen was such a weapon, heavy and simple, with a stout hand guard on the hilt that could be used as a knuckle duster if there were no room to swing the blade. The fighting sword used by officers was also comparatively short and curved, the 'hanger' type. In the course of time it would grow longer, straighter and less practical as it evolved into the modern pattern of naval officer's sword. The beautiful rapier-like 'dress' swords which appear in portraits of senior officers were solely for display. Midshipmen who were too

Below: Types of shot used by both sides during the war. From left to right: grapnel shot, spider shot (above), split chain shot (below), bar shot, chain shot, and ball. All of these, except for the ball shot, were designed to cut down the rigging of the enemy.

young and small to swing a cutlass would have a dirk instead, which might be either the familiar dagger-like weapon or a cut-down sword. In time this dirk became a symbol of the midshipman's rank.

Pistols, like sea service muskets, were merely rather plain and sturdy versions of the weapons used on land. Special features were added for convenience, such as carrying the ramrod in a stirrup below the barrel to prevent it from being dropped, and a belt hook along the lefthand side of the barrel. Hand

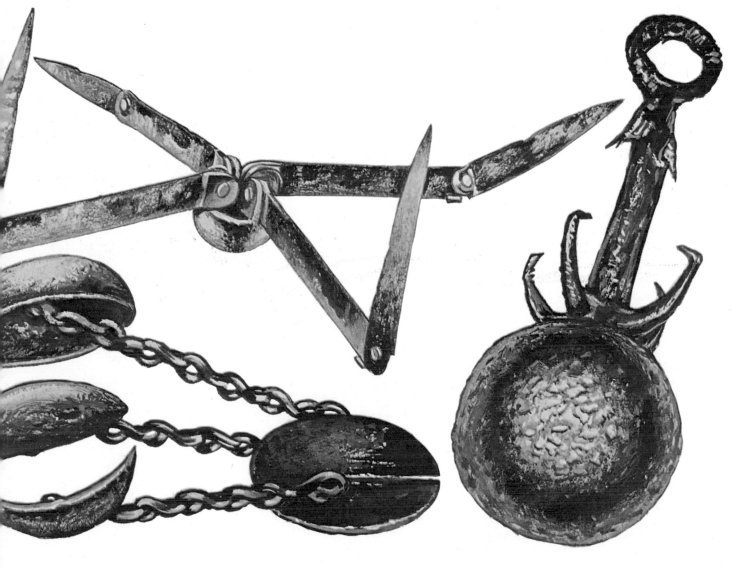

grenades were sometimes used in close actions, and were small hollow spheres filled with gunpowder, like shells, and ignited by hand. Parties in the fighting tops could cause great damage by throwing grenades down onto the enemy ship's deck, as the crew of the *Bonhomme Richard* did against the *Serapis*.

'Secret' Weapons

During the course of the Revolutionary War a number of new weapons and technical developments appeared, some of which were of lasting importance: A new type of gun was put into service; a number of minor innovations added greatly to the fighting power of the British fleet; the French and Spanish jointly produced some extraordinary bombardment ships; and the Americans invented two new weapons of lasting importance.

The Carronade

Early in 1779 the first example of an entirely new type of gun was cast by the Carron Iron Foundry in Scotland. Probably invented by General Melville, it was at first called the 'smasher', but soon became known by a name coined from its place of origin. Though the 'carronade' was shorter than an ordinary

Top left: Volley gun. With seven barrels each loaded with two balls, a devastating blast could cut a swathe through massed boarders.

Centre left: A musketoon.

Lower left: American brass barrelled swivel gun. Too heavy to be held and fired by the gunner, it was usually mounted on a bulwark.

Above: Depression carriage designed and built very rapidly for the defense of Gibraltar by the British. Its chief virtue was that it could fire downhill, unlike the normal ship-carriage.

Below: Pistol loading sequence. First a measure of powder was poured into the barrel, followed by a ball wrapped in a piece of cloth which had been soaked in tallow. The ball was rammed home firmly on the powder. Next the cock was pulled back to a half-cock position, and if required, the touch hole was cleaned or cleared with a pricker or piece of twine. A measure of fine priming powder was poured into the priming pan and the frizzen closed. In this state the gun was loaded but safe, as it could not fire in the half-cock position. When required to fire, the cock was pulled back to 'full cock' and the trigger was pulled, which allowed the cock to spring forward, scooping down the frizzen, which was being forced open at the same time. This allowed sparks from the contact of flint and steel to shower into the priming powder. This

flashed through the touch hole in the side of the barrel, igniting the main charge.
Right: John Paul Jones, by Noah Saunders.

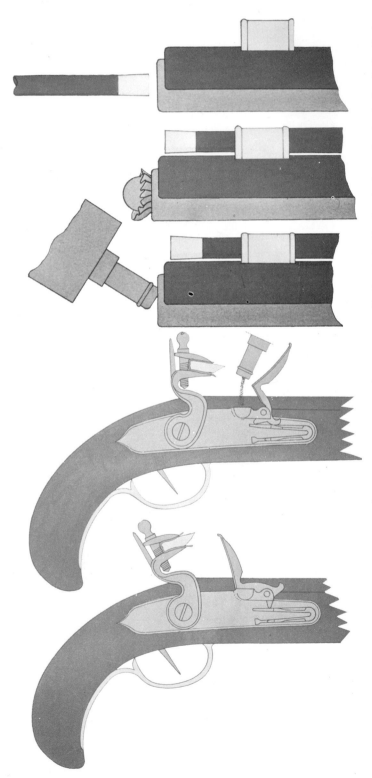

4-pounder, and a little lighter than a 12-pounder, it could fire a 68-pound shot. This was possible by using a small charge and a short barrel, and relying on the weight rather than the velocity of the shot to do damage. Because of the smaller charge, the walls of the barrel could be made comparatively thin, and this, combined with the shortness of the weapon, produced a gun with great power in relation to its weight.

For the British, whose preferred method of fighting was to get close to an enemy and then overwhelm him by rapid and heavy broadsides, this short-range cannon was the ideal weapon, particularly as it required a much smaller crew than a comparable cannon. The ease of operating the gun was helped by using a 'slide' carriage instead of the usual truck carriage. The recoil was absorbed and limited by the slide, and so the weapon took up less deck space than a conventional gun. Unlike a cannon, the carronade had a single trunnion underneath its barrel, pierced to fit into side bearings on the slide. This innovation allowed the weapon to be elevated and depressed by a screw in a threaded socket at the back of the barrel, and was a much more accurate method than using quoins and wedges. The side bearings which took the trunnion were mounted on a sliding bed, which in its turn slotted into a longer training bed. This training bed was attached by a vertical pin or 'pivot' to a base just inside the gun port of ship's side, and its rear end could be moved from side to side, running on two wooden trucks, to traverse the gun.

The carronade was indeed a fine example of engineering principles applied to gun design. Elevation and traversing were done with greater ease and with more accuracy than with the old wedges and tackles. The recoil was taken up by the friction between the slide and the traversing bed, though a breeching rope was still fitted as a back up. The carronade was so easy to use that in an action between the British frigate *Flora* and the French *Nymphe*, an 18-pounder manned only by the boatswain assisted by a boy played a vital part in winning the battle.

The Carron Company, anticipating the success of

the 'smasher', produced smaller copies, 24-, 18- and 12-pounders, and later 32-pounders, which were sold as soon as they were made. The new light weapon, with its small crews, was obviously ideal for merchant ships and privateers, and was immediately popular. The Admiralty was not slow in taking it up, either. Within six months of the first being made, a scale of armament using 12- and 18-pounder carronades for the different rates of warship had already been approved. By fitting carronades, armament was significantly increased at a relatively minor cost in extra weight, maneuverability and manpower.

At first there were a few teething troubles with the carronade, particularly the mounting, but these were rapidly overcome. By the beginning of 1781 there appear to have been 604 carronades in service with the British Navy, a highly creditable total, and one which shows that 18th century navies were not behind in taking up a technological improvement when they needed to. Until the end of the war no other navy had

Top: Powder tester to determine the strength and consistency of black gunpowder.
Centre: Spanish pistol with miquelet lock. Although awkward to operate, they were widely used in the Spanish service.
Right: Duckfoot pistol. Some had levers which enabled one barrel at a time to be fired. A favorite with masters of merchantmen, whose crews did not always understand discipline, these pistols fired a spread of bullets into a crowd of mutinous seamen.

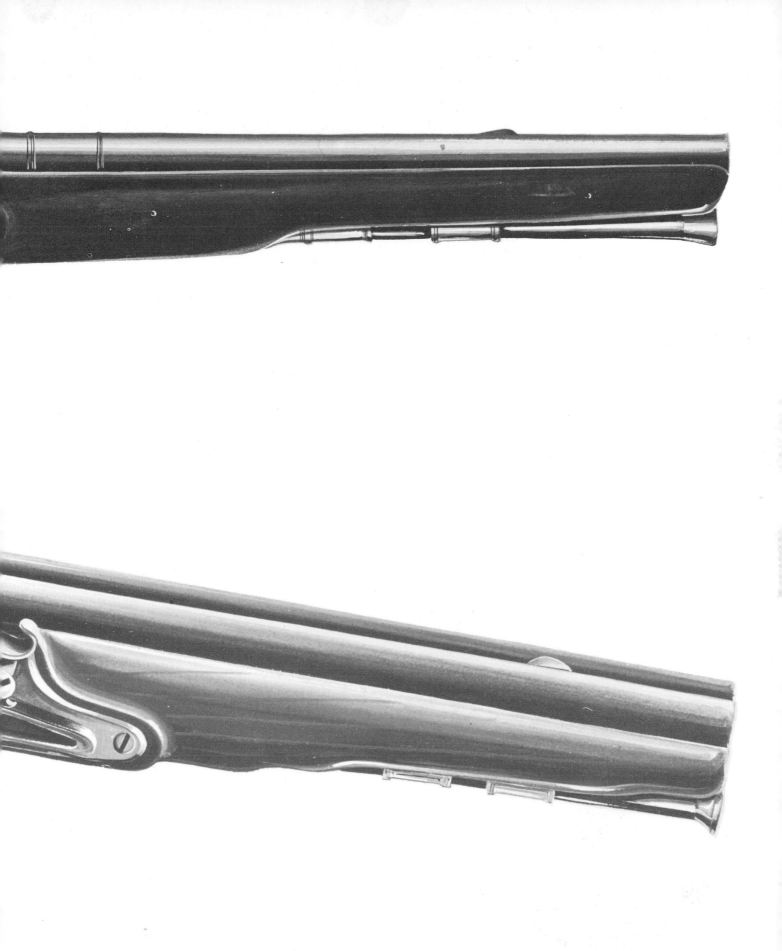

Top: A Dutch pistol, made by Penterman in 1705, but used in the Revolutionary War.
Above: A Joseph Stockl pistol, made in Germany, and used on Dutch ships.

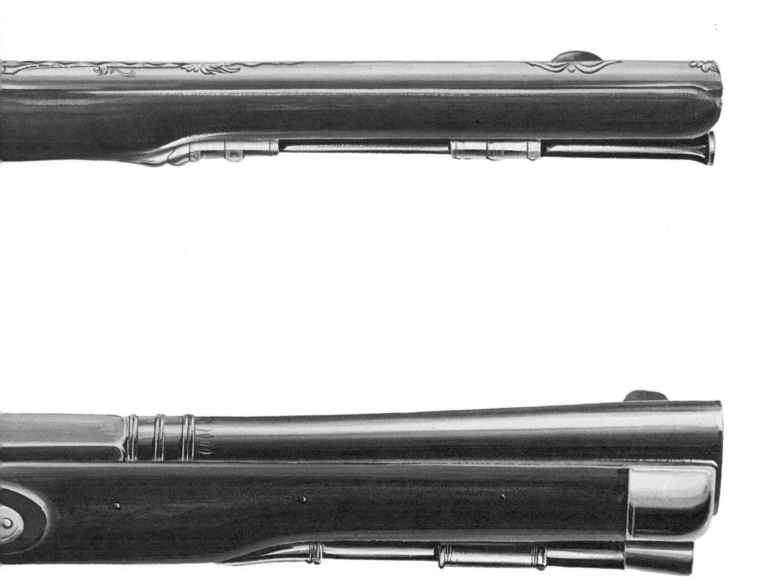

carronades, and the increase in firepower afforded by this weapon frequently tipped the balance in favor of the British in single-ship actions.

Gunnery improvements

At the same time, improvements were also being made to the conventional broadside guns. These were mainly the work of a Captain Douglas, who, as Flag Captain (i.e. Chief of Staff) to Admiral Rodney in the West Indies in the closing years of the war, was in a very good position to get his pet schemes adopted. None of them were particularly new ideas, but their adoption on a large scale made as much difference to the firepower of at least one ship in the British fleet at the vital, final Battle of the Saintes as did the new-fangled carronades.

The firing of a cannon by the traditional method of using a bit of old rope soaked in saltpetre (slowmatch) had always been an unreliable method, as was the transference of this light to the main charge by an uncertain trail of gunpowder. Using goose quills filled with fine powder had actually been tried in the Seven Years War, but for some reason it was discarded. Douglas revived this eminently satisfactory method of exploding the charge, and produced the initial spark from a flintlock mechanism, similar to that fitted to muskets and pistols for over a century. The increase in speed and reliability in 'priming' (preparing the firing) of a gun as a result of these improvements made possible a small but significant increase in the rate of fire.

Another improvement concerned gunlaying. One of the snags of mounting nearly all the guns on the broadside was that the effective angle over which the guns could fire was very restricted, an important consideration when trying to move down towards an

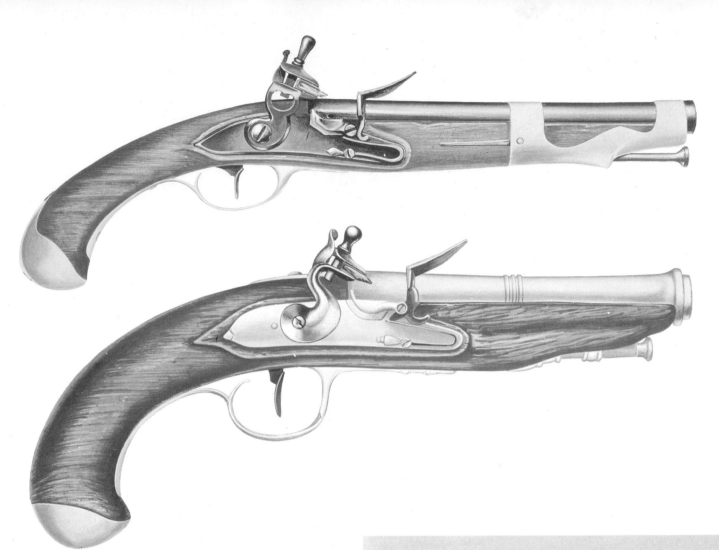

enemy fleet. Unless the approach angle was very shallow indeed one could not use one's own guns at all, while ships passing each other in opposite directions were lucky if they could exchange more than one broadside. Douglas, by clever repositioning of the training tackles, nearly doubled the angle of fire. A ship so fitted could now make a much quicker approach to an enemy while still keeping her under fire, a most important development for British fleets which normally believed in close action against French fleets which often were trying to avoid just that. When passing on opposite tacks, twice as many broadsides could be fired. These comparatively minor improvements thus meant a great increase in power for the British fleets towards the end of the war.

Coppering
Perhaps the most vital improvement in naval warfare was not at first sight a weapon at all. Yet it may well have made the difference between absolute defeat and the qualified victory with which Britain finally emerged. This improvement was the coppering of ships' bottoms.

Top and centre left: Two French naval pistols.
Below: Another variety of French naval pistol.
Bottom: Underwater defenses set in rivers and bays by the
Americans to prevent landings by British boats.

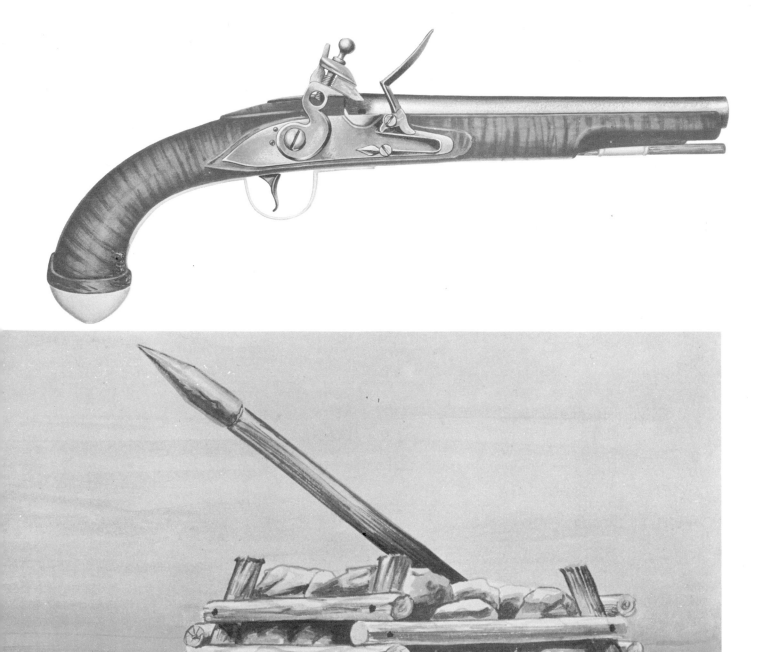

Right: Cannon flintlock. This enabled the sometimes unreliable method of linstock and touch hole ignition to be dispensed with. The lanyard release also enabled the gunner to be clear of the cannon.
Below: A 68-pdr. carronade.

When a ship had been in commission for some time, particularly in tropical waters, the number and size of the small creatures and vegetation which were attached to the bottom grew, and the increase in this marine growth led to an appreciable dropping off in speed, thanks to the increase in resistance. Also, small burrowing animals, Teredo worms, bored and ate their way into the timbers, gradually weakening the structure of the ship. If some way of stopping growth on the bottom and keeping the boring animals out could be found, there would be an effective increase in the life of ships, and vessels could keep up their speed without the necessity of having frequent dockings to scrape and burn off the growth on the bottom. This would be particularly important for the British Navy which tended to keep its ships at sea more than the French, who tended to keep their ships in harbor until their chosen moment, giving them, as often as not, a speed advantage over their rivals.

Lead sheathing had been tried as early as the time of Queen Elizabeth, but, though revived as a method several times, it was never very satisfactory. Lead was very heavy, not very strong, expensive, and liable to corrosion. By the middle of the 18th century an alternative method of sheathing was in general use. A loathsome concoction, usually made up of white lead, grease, tar and several other unpleasant ingredients, was spread on a thin layer of dead planks nailed to the bottom. This was not totally ineffective,

but the protection it gave did not last very long, and ships had to be docked with monotonous regularity for the remains of the sheathing to be stripped and replaced.

In 1761 copper sheathing was employed, for the first time, on the British 32-gun frigate *Alarm*. Two more vessels were given copper sheathing in 1764, but it was not until 1776 that the innovation began to catch on. In that year four ships were coppered, in 1777 nearly a dozen. By the end of the war there was hardly a ship in the British Navy which had not been coppered, and the French and Spanish were beginning to follow suit. The first French ship to be coppered was the frigate *Belle Poule* in 1777. Copper sheathing was expensive, but it proved to be the answer both to marine growth and to borers. This was because copper rapidly forms a layer of oxide on its surface, poisonous to most marine life and too slippery for plants to cling to.

For a while, until the enemy navies followed suit, fleets of coppered British ships could sail rings round their rivals, and could therefore force or avoid action at will. This temporary advantage was vital to the outnumbered and hard-pressed British Navy, and lasted until the end of the war.

Floating Batteries
One of the most important actions of the international war was the prolonged, though ultimately unsuccessful siege of Gibraltar by Spain and France. In 1782 the French and Spanish planned a great final assault to capture this provoking stronghold. An important element in their calculations was a new weapon. A French engineer, D'Arçon, designed a new type of floating battery intended to be proof against enemy gunfire, even the dreaded red hot shot. These were to be blockish, unwieldy craft, intended for one purpose only, and meant to be towed by boats. They were built on the hulls of old ships with a completely new appearance above water. They were lopsided, as only one flank was to be exposed to the enemy's fire. This side was three feet thick, with stout wooden

Below: Final sea action of the Revolutionary War between USS *Alliance* (under Captain John Barry) and HMS *Sybil* on 10 March 1783. Ironically *Alliance* was to be the last ship in the Continental Navy before being sold in June 1785.

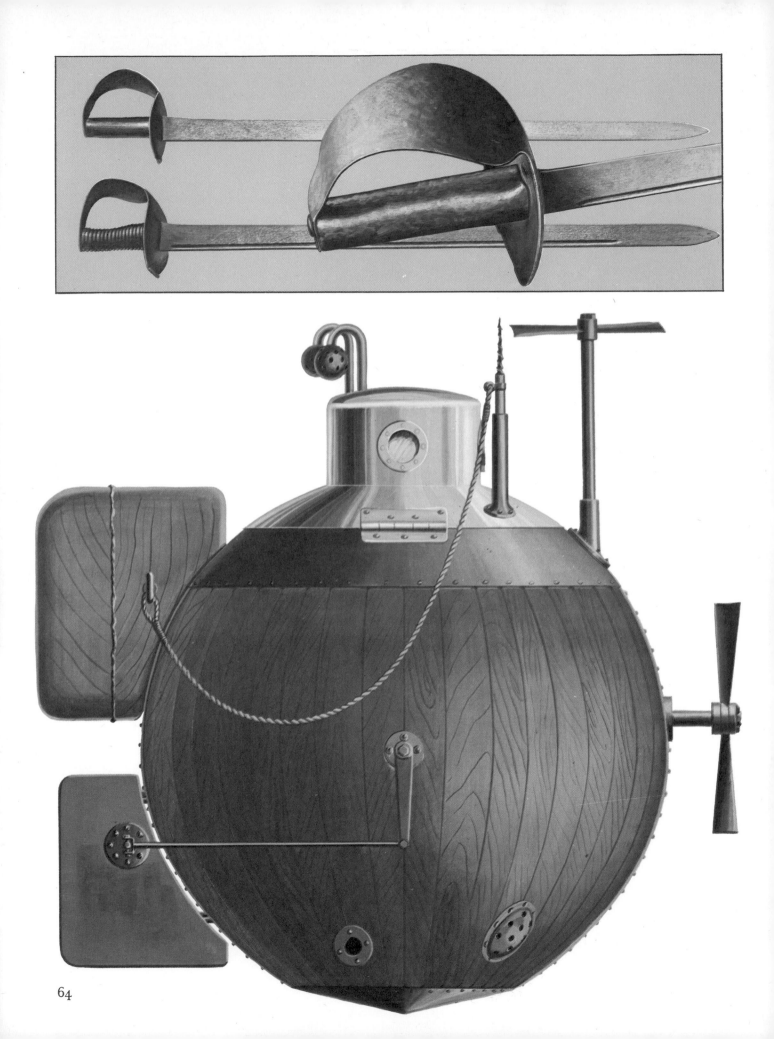

planking on inside and outside, the gap between being filled with a mixture of wet sand and cork. A network of water pipes ran through this to keep the side damp and to smother any outbreak of fire. In effect the batteries were armored, though not with metal. The weight of this thick side, and of the 36-pounders with which it was armed, was counterbalanced by ballast in the bilges on the other side of the hull. An ingenious roofing system was devised to dislodge any incendiary device which landed upon it.

Ten of these monstrous devices were prepared at Cadiz, and on 13 September 1782 they were towed into action, as part of a great combined assault on Gibraltar. The tremendous exchange of fire went on all day, but as night fell the guns of the fortress were seen to be winning the upper hand, the fire of the floating batteries slackened, and, one by one, they caught fire. Perhaps their designer was right in maintaining that their loss was due to insufficient trials and to lack of support from the other attacking forces who failed to provide the boats to extricate them. It is more likely that in a prolonged exchange of fire the ingenious defenses of the floating batteries were bound to be slowly overcome by the sheer number of hits. In any case, this secret weapon had failed, and Gibraltar remained British.

The Turtle

The most extraordinary inventions of the whole war were the work of a young American, David Bushnell, who, in conditions of considerable difficulty, not only produced the world's first combat submarine, but also pioneered the idea of sinking ships by *underwater*

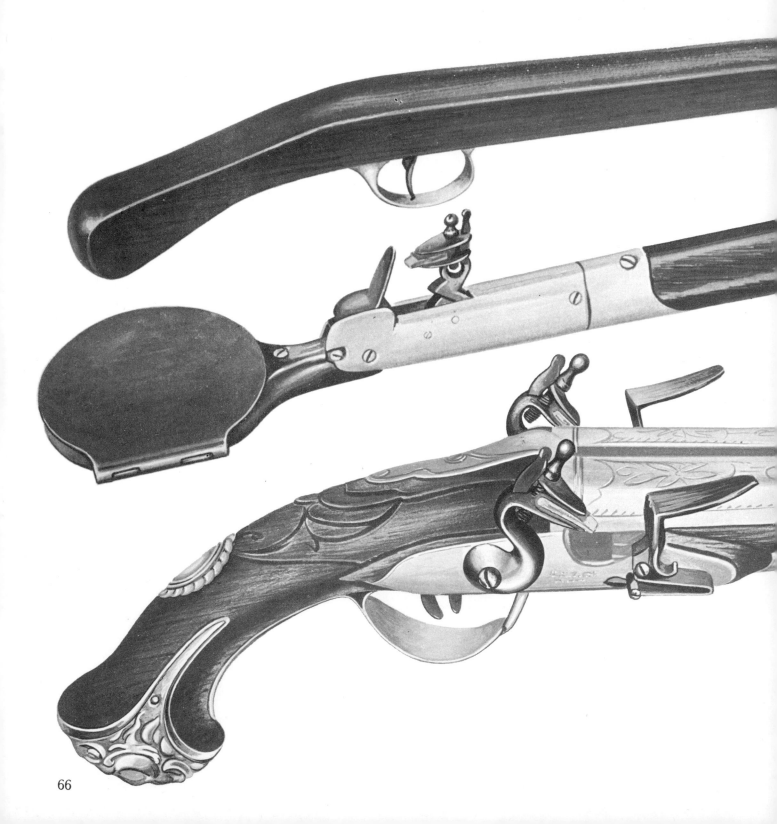

Below and centre: Two signal pistols. The pan was kept closed until the pistol was ready for use. Held level, the pan opened, and the pistol was ready to fire. Gunpowder with an excess of saltpetre, which caused a very white flame, was the mixture used in the pan.
Bottom: Double barrelled French naval pistol. Note the unusual brass lock on this weapon.

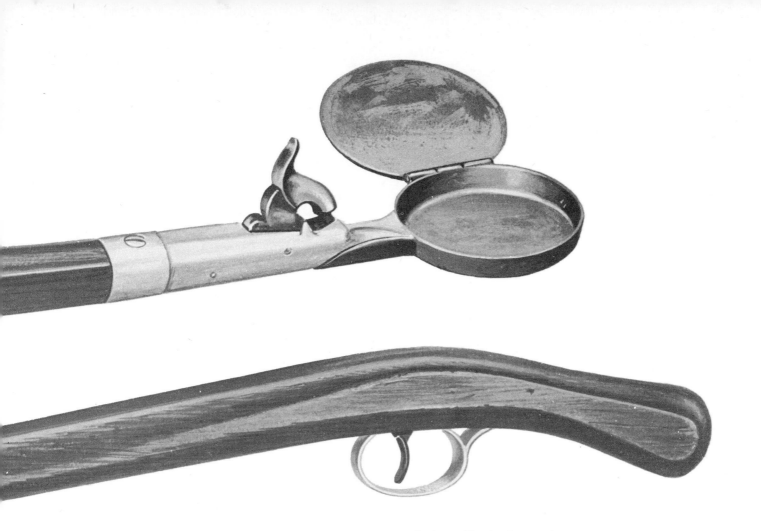

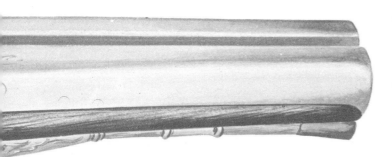

explosions. Exploding a charge next to the bottom of a ship is by far the most efficient way of sinking it, for ships were rarely sunk by gunfire alone in the 18th century. Bushnell had proved that gunpowder could be set off under water in the right conditions. He then had to work out a method of getting his charge near to the British ships which were lying off the port of New York in 1776.

His answer was to build a submarine which not only worked, but included a number of astonishingly modern features. It had a 'pressure hull' that looked like a chocolate Easter egg, or the shell of the turtle from which it took its name. There was an internal ballast tank, lead ballast which could be dropped in an emergency, and a snorkel breathing tube for the one-man crew. Like the midget submarines of World War II, the *Turtle* carried a detachable charge. This consisted of 150 pounds of gunpowder with a clock-work and flintlock fuse. The charge was attached to a screw which the operator was supposed to bore into the hull of the victim, and then detach from the sub-marine. Horizontal and vertical paddles were provided for propulsion and assistance in submerging and surfacing. The operator could look out of glass ports in a little 'conning tower' at the top of the *Turtle*. It was altogether a most ingenious design, and it

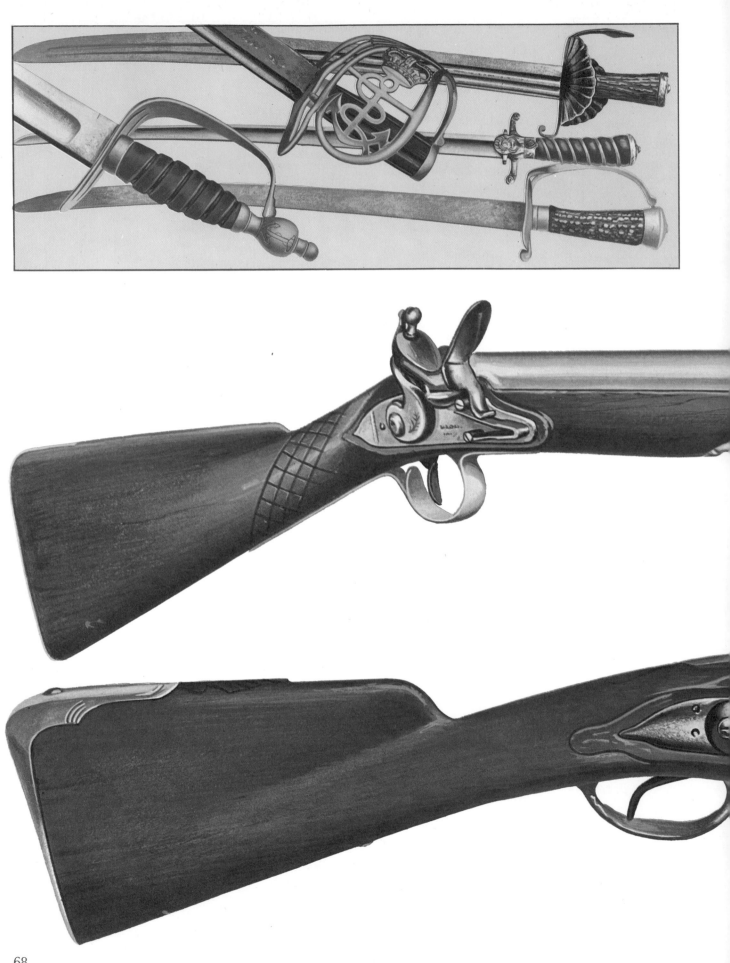

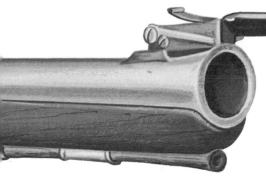

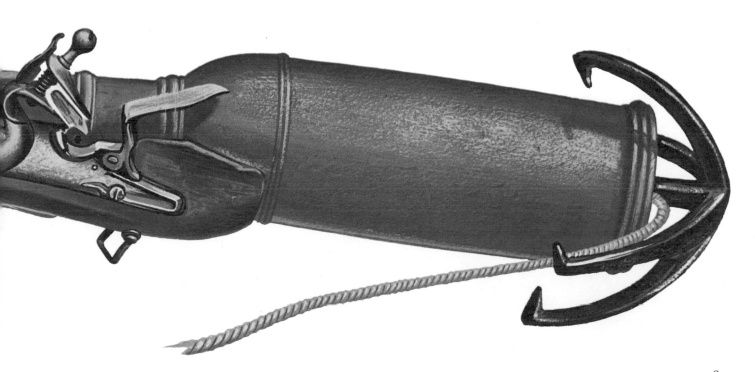

Top left: Hilts of naval swords.
Above: Surgeon's tools. As many men died under the surgeon's hands from shock as those immediately killed in action.
Left: Blunderbuss with spring bayonet.
Bottom: A Dutch hand mortar with grapnel.

Below: Bullet molds.
Centre: The American fleet under Commodore Hopkins chasing the British frigate HMS *Glasgow* off Long Island in April 1776.
Right: Dirks were held in the left hand during hand-to-hand fighting on ships while a pistol or sword was held in the right hand. If the seaman lost his sword or when his pistol needed reloading, he could fight on with his dirk, which sometimes were made from cut-down or damaged swords.

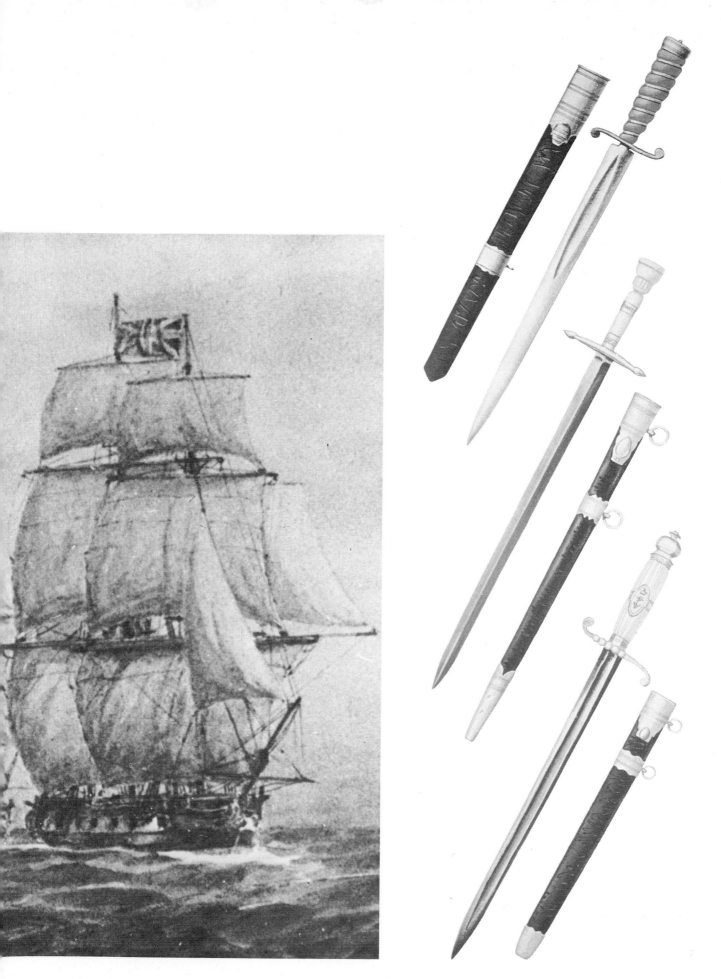

actually worked. The main snag was that it relied entirely on the strength and ingenuity of one man who would have to propel, navigate and dive the boat, as well as carrying out the maneuvers needed to attach the charge and start the fuse.

The incredible thing is not that Sergeant Ezra Lee (who volunteered to make the attack on the British flagship *Eagle* when Bushnell had found the task beyond his strength) failed, but that this fantastically brave and fit young man so nearly succeeded. He was towed to within a couple of miles of the British ships, then slipped down-tide. He overshot and had to work up against the tide until he got alongside the *Eagle*. He failed to attach the charge to her hull, despite making two attempts, and had to give up. He finally got back to join his friends after slipping the explosive charge, which gave the pursuing British guard-boats a nasty shock.

The reason why he failed to drive the screw of the charge into *Eagle*'s hull is usually stated to be that the ship's copper bottom prevented this. However the *Eagle* had not been coppered at this stage of the war, so this is obviously wrong. Perhaps he was trying to screw into one of the iron nails holding the wooden sheathing on, or perhaps even one of the rudder fastenings. In addition, it must be remembered that Lee was working at night, looking through thick glass ports which were unlikely to be of very good quality, and further obscured by misting up.

It is, however, even more likely that poor Lee just found the wooden bottom itself too tough. After all he had been working in a confined space in conditions of extreme stress for some time before he reached the *Eagle*. Carbon dioxide from his exhaled air would be making him progressively more stupefied (Bushnell reported suffering from bad headaches and being incapacitated for some time after operating the *Turtle*, the classic signs of carbon dioxide poisoning). But above all, because it is extremely difficult to exert pressure on anything underwater without pushing oneself backwards; the only way Lee could have exerted enough pressure to drive the screw which

Above: English short Brown Bess (Sea Service).
Below: French Charleville musket (Sea Service).

Below: The Battle of the Kegs took place in 1778 when Bushnell, the inventor of *Turtle*, decided to send wooden kegs loaded with gunpowder down the Delaware River. They failed to hit their British targets when these floating mines were spotted. After the first one blew up a guard boat, to the amusement of the Americans, the British ships avoided the kegs. The victims of the blast were among the earliest casualties in the history of minesweeping operations.

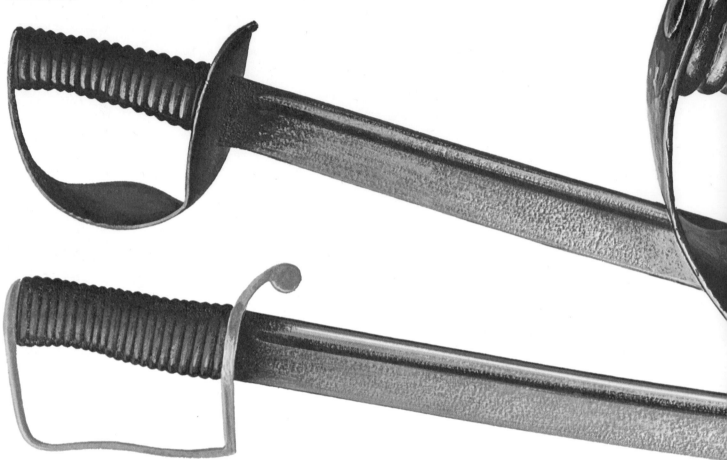

attached the charge to the target would have been to operate the propulsion screw simultaneously——a very difficult procedure even for a fresh man.

Mines

After inventing the submarine as a weapon of war, the brilliant Bushnell turned to inventing the first true submarine mines. In 1777 Bushnell launched another attack against the British, this time operating in the Connecticut River. By 'throwing a machine against the side by means of a line, he apparently sank a small schooner instead of the intended target, the *Cerberus*.

In 1778 Bushnell renewed his efforts by sending a series of kegs full of gunpowder down the Delaware against British ships. These kegs contained a spring-lock designed to go off when the 'mine' touched an obstacle. The invisible kegs were suspended below floats which gave them the necessary buoyancy. Unfortunately for the attack, the kegs were released too far away from the target, and were additionally held up by ice in the river. They should have hit the British ships in the dark, but instead they were spotted in the morning light. Guard boats were sent to investigate them, and one which became too curious was blown up with the loss of four of the crew killed and the rest wounded. They must have the melancholy distinction of being the earliest casualties caused by minesweeping operations. The rest of the mines missed their intended targets because the British ships had moved inshore to avoid the ice which had already delayed the mines. However, not unnaturally, there was a period of panic after the first explosion which gave the Americans some amusement, and the incident was given the title of 'the Battle of the Kegs'.

Despite some other similar attacks which had even less success, Bushnell's rôle as a major naval inventor came to an end. Many of his ideas and much of the credit for his brilliant innovations were taken over

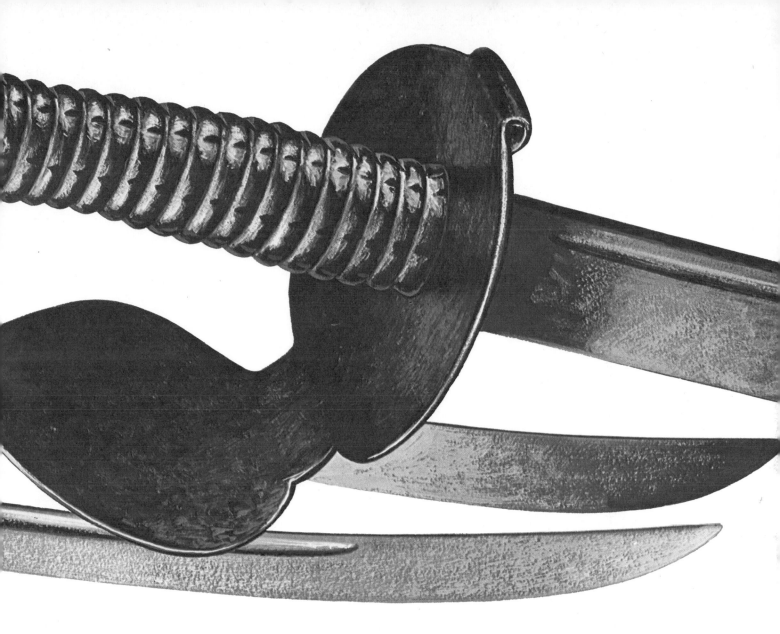

by later men, such as Fulton. We can now, however, see him as the true father of modern undersea warfare.

Admiralties and Dockyards

Behind each navy lay an organization of greater or lesser complexity. Warships were then the most complex single items built by man, and the construction, maintenance and direction of these ships required a correspondingly large and complicated system of support and management. A large navy was the largest single economic and industrial organization in the country, the biggest employer of labor, and the most expensive to run.

The major French dockyards were at Brest, Toulon and Boulogne. The largest naval power, Britain, had five major dockyards. Portsmouth, Plymouth and Chatham were the biggest, but the Thames yards, Deptford and Woolwich, and Sheerness were large plants in their own right. All these yards both built

and refitted ships. They were backed up by a network of dockyards overseas, almost entirely concerned with the maintenance and refitting of the local squadrons. The major foreign bases were Gibraltar and Minorca (the latter lost during the war) in the Mediterranean, Antigua and Jamaica in the West Indies, Halifax in North America and Bombay in India. If necessary a dockyard organization could be set up in a captured port, as was done at New York. In general these overseas yards would carry an adequate stock of naval stores for repairs, and could even cope with such major matters as coppering if necessary, though most of this was done in Britain. Provided the skilled labor was available temporary dockyards could be set up, as the British did at the northern end of Lake Champlain and Benedict Arnold at Skenesboro' at the southern end of the same lake. The British obtained their skilled carpenters and shipwrights from the fleet; the Americans from the New England ports.

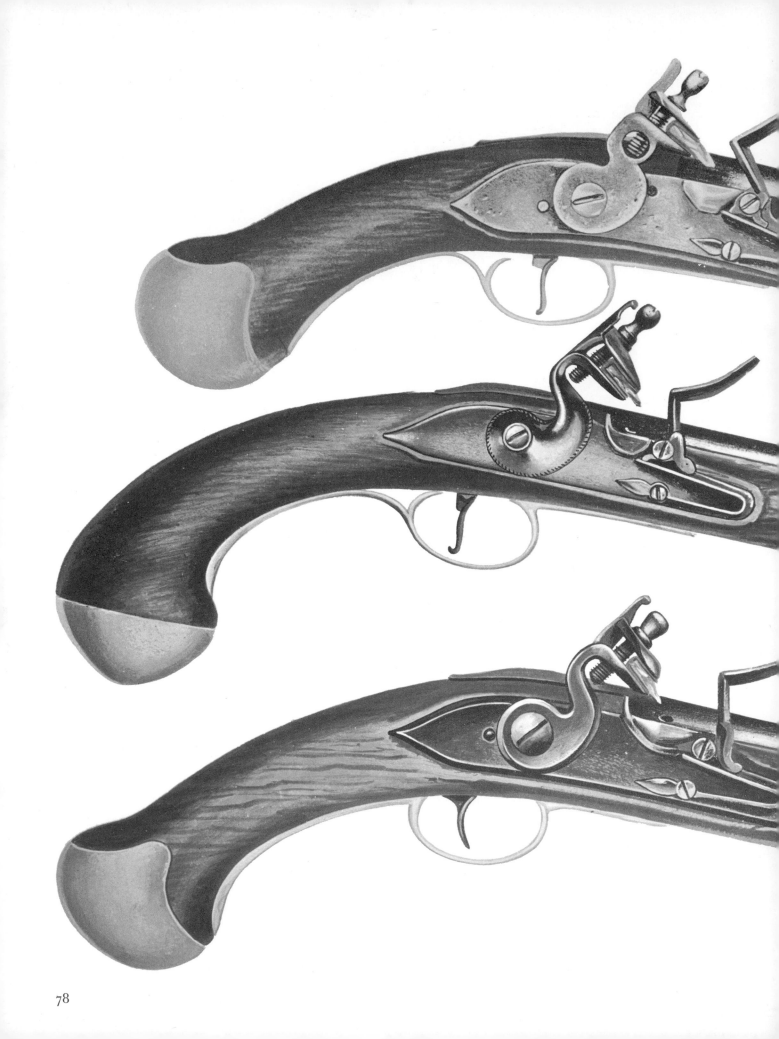

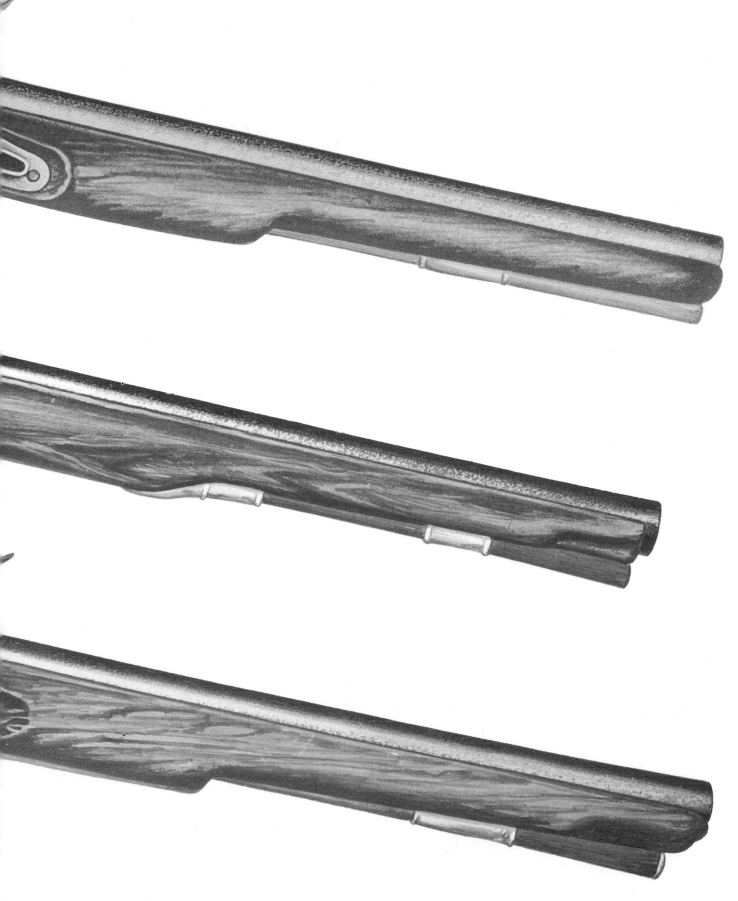

Opposite: French Marine. When, on 14 August 1779, the Continental Navy Commodore John Paul Jones sailed for operations in British coastal waters, his squadron had among its complement a force of 137 French Marines. His own ship the *Bonhomme Richard* included Irishmen from the French Regiment of Marine Artillery of the French service, and French officers of Marines.

Dress: Dark blue coat with red facings and cuffs with white turnbacks. Waistcoat, gaiters and breeches——white.

Right: Privateer. At the outbreak of hostilities the revolutionaries were without a naval force. Merchant ships suitable for warlike enterprises received extra ordnance suitable for ocean-raiders. Their officers recruited privateer crews. A privateer was little more than a licensed pirate, bearing a commission or letter of marque issued by warring governments. Congress began issuing letters of marque in March 1776. British privateers also sailed under letters of marque from London. The American privateers were of mixed nationalities, some hailing from the Caribbean, the former home waters of Kidd, Blackbeard and other notorious terrors of the seas. Besides harassing the enemy, privateers produced many fine officers for the Continental service and the future United States Navy.

Opposite right: John Barry, Captain of USS *Alliance*, which fought the last sea battle of the Revolutionary War against the British in 1783.

The Men

Each navy solved the problem of finding the huge number of men required for manning their ships in different ways. All European nations used one form or another of conscription, as the great numbers needed could not be obtained except by compulsion. This conscription concentrated on those subjects who were already involved in maritime occupations, although in dire emergency landsmen might be roped in as well. The French operated a system known as the '*Inscription Maritime*', by which all seamen, fishermen and boatmen were registered and liable to be called up for the fleet.

In Britain too, there was a theoretical obligation for all seamen to serve the King in time of war. However, the method used to conscript them was much more rough and ready than that used by the French. The method used was the infamous 'press gang'. It was certainly unjust, inhuman and totally inefficient, yet it is important to realize that it was a recognized precondition of anyone becoming a seaman that he

Below: The *Bonhomme Richard* engaging HMS *Serapis* on 23 September 1779. The stern of *Bonhomme Richard* can be seen to the left behind *Serapis*. To the right is USS *Alliance* firing her third broadside.

was liable to be pressed in wartime, and that landsmen were rarely pressed unless they were criminals or
bankrupts. Certainly seamen always did their best to
avoid the press gang and to obtain the prized certi-
ficate of exemption.

It is not surprising that thousands of conscripts
deserted when they could. The 'Inscription Maritime'
was at least as unpopular as the press. Indeed it
is possible that the English seaman preferred the
lottery of the press gang, which he might at least
avoid through his own efforts, than the bureaucratic
tyranny of the French system. Nothing, however, can
detract from the sheer nastiness of the system of
pressing men. Gangs of seamen would go out under
the command of junior officers in the streets of sea-
ports, raid the taverns and doss-houses, often helped
by cordons of troops and club reluctant sailors into
submission. The favored method of preventing escape
was to remove belt or braces from trousers. Boats
would also be sent out to take men off returning
merchant ships, and there were times when regular
battles were fought by crews reluctant to join the
navy. The whale ships of Hull were particularly
well known for this.

Once taken into the navy from the press or the jails,
the new recruits would be kept aboard a hulk or
tender until they could be put on board the ships that
were crying out for men. Towards the end of the war,
pressure from some progressive doctors caused the
Admiralty to introduce a number of 'receiving hulks'.
In these the new men could be kept in relatively
comfortable surroundings, issued clean clothing, made
to clean themselves, and be kept in quarantine for a
while to make sure that they did not introduce
infectious diseases to the ships of the fleet. The incidence of epidemics, very dangerous in the crowded
conditions of wooden ships, dropped immediately.

By no means all the men in the major navies were
conscripts. Even in the worst periods of the war, when
the British Navy needed men desperately, only half
the total were pressed. This is to a certain extent a
misleading figure, as sometimes pressed men were

Right: Boatswain, Royal Navy, 1775–83. The boatswain was in charge of the sails, rigging, anchors, cables, boats and everything which pertained to the working of the ship. His mates were hand-picked from the best seamen. Together they insured that commands were properly obeyed, if necessary with the aid of the dreaded cat o' nine tails and a knotted rope end, illustrated here——a 'colt' or 'starter'.

Above right: The first salute to the Stars and Stripes at sea, 1778; John Paul Jones in *Ranger*.

Far right: Leadsman. Much of the early navigation was dependent upon the sandglass, reel, log chip and the lead. The lead had a hollow in the end. Before casting the lead the hollow was filled with tallow, so that samples of the sea bed could be examined. The line was marked at regular intervals with signs which could easily be identified under adverse conditions: two strips of leather at two fathoms, three at three fathoms, a white duck at five, a piece of red bunting at seven, a piece of leather with a hole in it at ten, and so on.

given the chance to 'volunteer' after they had been caught; this meant higher pay, and many took this way out. But there were certain attractions for genuine volunteers, particularly in the frigates, ships more likely to make captures and obtain much-coveted 'prize money'. In any fleet, they rarely needed to take conscripts, especially if the captain was known to be humane and lucky.

Because the infant American Navy disdained conscription, recruitment was small. Discipline aboard ships of the Continental Navy was only slightly less harsh than in the navies of Europe; pay was erratic, low (top pay for a Captain was only $60 per month) and issued in the dubious Continental currency; and the American government's policy about sharing prize money with crews was, to say the least, uncompetitive. Small wonder that potential volunteers preferred the lure of higher profits and an easier life offered by the privateers. The Navy resorted to appeals to patriotism and the proffering of short-term enlistments, but in many cases recruitment techniques were only a few steps removed from outright shanghaiing. A contemporary sailor reported the manning of a frigate: 'Upwards of 330 men were carried, dragged or driven on board, of all kinds, ages and descriptions, in all the various states of intoxication'.

Marines

An important part of the crews of most ships were detachments of marines, soldiers especially enlisted to serve on board ship to provide the disciplined nucleus for sentry duty, landing parties and musket-fire in battle. They also performed the function of ship's police, and were the chief barrier against mutiny.

The British Marines, descended from the original Lord Admiral's Regiment of 1664, had been under the control of the Admiralty from 1747, and formed a substantial part of the fleet. In 1774, before war broke out, the official strength of the Navy was 16,000 men (it had just been reduced from 20,000), of whom about 4500 were Marines. In the middle of the war,

in 1781, the British Parliament voted to provide for 90,000 men in the Navy, 20,000 of whom were to be Marines. Of course these numbers were optimistic, and never quite attained.

Their nearest equivalents in the European navies were the Dutch Marines, founded in the same year, and with an equally proud history (the first action fought was against each other). The French, on the other hand, made a regular practice of drafting infantry regiments for marine service, as did the Spaniards.

The Americans founded their own Marines in the course of the war, and the detachment on board the *Bonhomme Richard* distinguished themselves in action against the *Serapis*. But it would be many years before this famous military force came into its own.

Discipline, Conditions of Service

In ships full of conscripted men discipline was, of necessity, harsh. Strict discipline was particularly necessary in the early weeks of a commission when there was a large proportion of non-seamen. The crew had to be welded into a team capable of doing all the complicated tasks of working the ship and firing the guns, and continuing to do them fast and automatically even when frightened.

Slow workers would be encouraged by petty officers equipped with rope's ends or canes. These would be used to 'start' laggards. Such unofficial punishment was backed up by the despotic power of the Captain. He was absolute master of the fate of his crew and officers, having, quite literally, the power of life and death. The degree of discipline enforced depended on the individual Captain. Some were sadists, others hardly used the lash at all; the majority were strict, but usually just men. Lashing a man with the cat-o'-nine tails was the usual major punishment, a brutal and degrading punishment in which the victim was tied to a grating and then flogged with a whip made with nine strands, all of them being knotted. Wielded by a Bosun's Mate, this could strip the skin from a man's back, and in extreme cases even lay bare the bones. The 'cat' would be freshly made for each occasion, for obvious hygienic reasons. Traditionally it was the victim himself who made it up. Theoretically the number of lashes were limited, but the limitation was often ignored. Floggings had to be recorded in the ship's log, and logs of different ships show great variation in the number and scale of floggings. This of course depended on the state of morale and obedience of the ship's company just as much as on the predilections of the Captain. In most ships it would only be the bad characters, and perhaps, the really unlucky who were flogged; the majority of seamen probably went through their years in the Navy without ever having their backs scarred by the 'cat'.

The ultimate sanction was death by hanging, a punishment usually invoked for cowardice, or for threatening or striking a superior. Virtually a death sentence but very rarely awarded, was the British sentence of 'flogging round the fleet', sending an offender round the ships of the fleet in a boat, with a specific number of lashes being laid on as the boat passed each ship. Like the death sentence this could only be awarded by a court martial.

Though 18th century naval discipline appears barbarous, we must see it in the context of its time. So far as we can find out, most contemporary sailors seem to have taken it for granted. What they usually objected to was not the system itself, but abuses of the system, the occasional brutal captain or the crooked or

Overleaf: The Battle off the Virginia Capes in which the French fleet under Admiral de Grasse prevented a British fleet under Admiral Graves from entering Chesapeake Bay and relieving General Cornwallis' trapped British Army at Yorktown. The sea battle took place on 5 September 1781. It was hardly a classic fight, but it was the most important naval victory of the war for the French. Soon after the fall of Yorktown negotiations for peace began.

sadistic petty officer. The quality of life afloat had, after all, to be compared with the quality of life ashore. And life ashore for the lower classes could be very grim indeed. In France and Spain the nobility held almost unlimited power over lesser mortals, and British courts could impose a death sentence for the theft of a handkerchief. At least sailors were usually fed, and paid, even though not very well. Americans perhaps had less need to escape the rigors of life ashore by going to sea, but they had another, more positive motive for doing so. They were fighting for a cause.

The average professional seaman, like his modern equivalent, was usually a friendly and gregarious soul, fond of strong drink and chasing women whenever he could as a reaction to confinement on board ship. A 'Run ashore' was a chance to 'blow' all the hard-earned money in a glorious drunken spree. The sad thing was that with so many pressed men on board, and the incidence of desertion so high, shore leave was hardly ever granted. In wartime as soon as one ship came into dockyard hands at the end of a commission or for refit, her crew would immediately be grabbed for filling the complements of other ships, with rarely a chance of setting foot ashore in between. As soon as war ended the Navy would be cut down ruthlessly, and the vast majority of seamen were thrown out of work. There was no pension scheme for injured, out of work or aged seamen, except for those lucky enough to become Greenwich Pensioners at the Royal Naval Hospital.

Crews were necessarily divided into two main categories, the skilled 'able seamen' and the unskilled 'landsmen'. The latter would normally be employed on deck, pulling and straining on ropes to order, providing the power for tasks nowadays performed by auxiliary machinery. These were the 'waisters', the men employed in the waist of the ship, and would include those too old, too unfit or too stupid to be used in the rigging. The trained seamen were superbly competent acrobats, capable of working in the dangerous and vertiginous task of taking in sails out of the

yards, many feet above the deck. The aristocracy, the fittest and most agile of the younger men were the 'topmen', those who worked on the higher sails and masts and the best of the topmen were those employed on the foremast, the 'foretopmen'. Older or less agile skilled men would have such jobs as 'captain' of a gun.

With the never-ceasing demands for hard physical work and moving of heavy weights, it is not surprising that the chief occupational injury was hernia. With the difficulty of drying wet clothes and the constantly damp atmosphere, rheumatism was also a common complaint. Living on a monotonous diet of ship's biscuit, salt meat and little else it is not surprising that vitamin deficiency diseases, of which the worst and best known was scurvy, were rife, particularly on long voyages. Though the use of fresh fruit in combating scurvy had been known to Sir John Hawkins 200 years earlier, it was not until after the end of the Revolutionary War that the Royal Navy, under the prodding of that great doctor, Sir James Lind, finally adopted the use of citrus fruit juice (first lemon, then lime juice) and at once removed the whole problem.

Anyone who has visited HMS *Victory* or the USS *Constitution*, and has visualized the lower decks with the full crew living aboard will realize just how cramped life was for a seaman. If he was lucky, he had a space 18 inches broad to sling his hammock at night. The sight of several hundred hammocks gently swinging in the low space between decks must have been an impressive one, and so must the aroma emanating from massed, sweating, unwashed humanity. In daytime the hammocks would be taken down and stowed; in battle they would be placed in rails on top of the bulwarks as a bullet-proof barrier. In between each gun was a mess table, a plank slung from the 'deckhead' (the sailor's word for the ceiling) off which the groups of sailors ate. At other times the table would be triced up against the deckhead, leaving the entire length of the decks uncluttered except for the guns, the capstans, and the cabin bulkheads.

Below: The schooner *Hannah* was owned by John Glover of Marblehead, Massachusetts, and she was the first armed vessel fitted out in the service of the United States, 5–7 September 1775.

Below: The *Serapis,* under the command of Captain Richard Pearson, under fire from *Bonhomme Richard.*

In the Navy the place where bowels or bladder are emptied is still known as the 'head'. In our period the 'heads' were still the actual head of the ship, the space just behind the figurehead. Originally the three rails, one below another, which curve so beautifully and ornamentally round from the figurehead to the ship's side, were for placing the back, bottom and feet respectively. The keen-eyed viewer of old marine paintings can sometimes spot a seaman in this position with his trousers down. There were also 'seats of ease' in the little grating platform between the rails. In bad weather this position in the bows became unusable, and the 'lee chains' (the small platforms where the shrouds were attached to the side of the hull, on the side of the ship opposite to where the weather was coming from), would be used. However it is not surprising that the bilges, the inner bottom of the hull, soon became a noisome breeding ground for infection.

Petty and Warrant Officers

It is always said that the backbone of any service is its long-service NCOs. This was as true of the 18th century as it is today. The junior noncoms were the captains of the tops and the guns, which were positions rather than ranks. The seniors were the various specialist warrant officers and their 'mates'. The 'Boatswain' or 'Bo'sun' was in charge of the seamen, the Carpenter was responsible for the structure of the ship, and the Purser ran the pay and the provision of food and clothing. Pursers had a bad reputation for dishonesty, but as they were expected to run their side of the ship as a private business this is hardly surprising. The tasks and responsibilities of the cook and the gunner are self-evident. The navigation and sailing of the ship came to a great extent under the 'sailing master' or 'master'. This was a hangover from the Middle Ages, when a merchant ship was taken over to serve as a warship and her master and crew came with her, but a soldier would be put in charge of the vessel to fight her. He would become the 'captain', but the master continued to sail and navigate

Below: Gunner. The gunner was in charge of the magazines, the manufacture of cartridges and shot, and the instruction of gun captains and their crews. The illustration shows molten metal being poured into a brass bullet mold with four cavities for different sizes of shot.
Opposite left: Captain, Royal Navy, 1775–83. Officers varied as much as their crews. Some were accomplished in seamanship and navigation, some incompetent owing their promotion to influence. Some were brutal, some stupid, others kindly—
—authority produced despotism and solitude. The captain lived alone, ate alone, planned alone and walked his quarterdeck alone. He was ultimately responsible for his subordinates and the ship. The three-year seniority of the captain illustrated is indicated by the twelve buttons arranged in twos on the lapels. The coat was blue, with blue facings, cuffs and collar. Waistcoat, breeches and hose were white.
Opposite right: Ship's carpenter. He had to be a competent craftsman, capable of building a ship's boat or a new mast. In charge of all repairs, he informed the captain of the state of the ship's hull, masts, yards and decks. He sounded the ships well and regularly to check the leakage, and insured that the pumps were clean and in good working order. In battle he and his mates plugged shot holes and made whatever repairs possible.

the ship. The distinction between the 'gentlemen' who fought, and the 'tarpaulin', the professional seaman who operated the ship, had diminished over the years, the 'gentleman' becoming the naval officer, quite competent himself to sail and navigate as well as fight. The master had fallen in status to being a mere adviser, though a senior and usually well-regarded one. In wartime many masters came in from the Merchant Service where they had been captains or mates.

Masters, Carpenters, Gunners, etc., held 'warrants', pieces of paper giving them their position, and were normally appointed by an Admiralty or its equivalent. The 'Commissions' which officers held were similar pieces of paper, but signed by the King or Congress, not the Admiralty, as befitted their higher status. They and their 'Mates' (assistants) were permanently attached to particular ships, staying with their ships as a skeleton crew even when she was out of commission and laid up in reserve.

Officers

The mark of the 18th century naval officer was that he held a commission from his monarch or, in the American case, from Congress. There were three main European ranks, Lieutenant, Captain and Admiral. The Americans counted Midshipmen, Masters, Lieutenants and Captains, but their service was too small to include Admirals. Before becoming an officer a boy served for a while as a kind of cadet with warrant officer status, in other words as a 'midshipman', though in the British Navy he might actually join as a 'volunteer' and become a midshipman later. Most midshipmen were boys or youths of 13 to 20 years of age, but some older men found themselves still in the 'gunroom', the midshipmen's mess, usually because of failure in examinations or lack of patronage.

'Patronage' is one of the most important keywords for understanding the 18th century. If you wanted a post or promotion, you tried to find an influential man who would support your efforts to obtain it.

Overleaf: The invasion of New Providence Island in the Bahamas on 3 March 1776. The initial objective of the Continental sailors and Marines was Fort Montagu, in the left background. Close by, offshore, were the small vessels used to transport the landing force near the beach. They were two captured sloops, the schooner *Wasp* and the sloop *Providence*.

Below: Master, Royal Navy. The highest ranking of men who usually held their rank by warrant rather than by commission was the sailing master. He was responsible for sailing the ship, trimming the sails and taking the vessel into battle. He was expected to know navigation and did survey work noting his findings on the charts. He supervized the writing of the ship's log and taught the midshipmen. Aiding him were one or more master's mates.

Dress: Coat, facings, cuffs and collar——blue; waistcoat, breeches and stockings——white; Illustrated with speaking trumpet and small sword.

Your 'patron' might do this for services rendered, financial or political, or because of family or local connections, or just because he was impressed by your competence. However, young Horatio Nelson began life in the Navy with an advantage which had nothing to do with natural brilliance, his uncle being Comptroller of the Navy.

For officers the most difficult barrier to surmount was that between lieutenant and captain. To become a lieutenant you had to pass an examination in seamanship, but once you were a lieutenant only patronage or good luck could get you any higher. 'Luck' could include being a junior lieutenant in a ship when all your superiors were killed or disabled, or the possibility of distinguishing yourself in a cutting-out expedition, or an independent command. Lieutenants who commanded sloops and other small vessels were known as 'master and commander' (not to be confused with the 'master' who was a warrant officer, as we have seen) or 'lieutenants in command'. This was the origin of the modern ranks of Commander and Lieutenant Commander in the US and British Navies, and of their equivalents in other navies.

Once a captain, promotion was by seniority, though patronage and luck still determined what sort of commands a man got. There were three ranks for admirals——Rear Admirals, Vice Admirals and Admirals (or as the French had it, *contre-amiral*, *vice-amiral*, and *amiral*). Senior captains in command of more than one ship were known as Commodores, but this was not a true rank. British admirals were also divided into three lists, 'of the White', 'the Red' or 'the Blue'. This was a way of describing seniority within each rank, and dated from the time when the whole British Navy operated as one fleet, divided into vanguard, main fleet and rearguard, each flying a distinctively colored flag.

Most naval officers came from the middle class, descended from merchants, tradesmen, clerks and the like, though there were many 'naval families'. The Navy was not as fashionable as the Army, but there were a number of aristocrats among the officers.

Right: American Captain of Marines. This famous, hard-fisted, hard-drinking body of men took part in Hopkins' expedition to the Bahamas in March 1776 and in many other marine and land operations. The Marines wore green jackets in this period, but in 1797 the basic color of the uniform was changed to blue.

During wartime expansion some merchant navy officers would come into the navy as 'masters' or 'masters' mates', and a few of these achieved officer rank, like James Cook. Promotion from the lower deck was very rare, but not totally unknown.

Commissions were given for individual ships, a new one was issued for each appointment, and when a ship was 'paid off' her crew would be dismissed and her officers go on half-pay, if there was not another ship to transfer to immediately. In peacetime most officers were on half-pay, and many served in merchant ships or took other jobs to get more money.

At this time uniforms were for officers only, and were a relatively new innovation for them. Seamen might appear fairly uniform if the purser's 'slop chest' contained clothes of the same type, and wealthy captains might outfit their boat's crew in a special uniform, but normally seamen wore what clothes were available, though there was a preference for loose white trousers and striped shirts. In most navies the officer's uniform tended to be a modified form of the civilian dress of the time——blue coats and breeches and tricorn hats, with badges of rank appearing as epaulettes; braiding on cuffs, collars and lapels; and varying styles of facings.

The Techniques of sea-fighting

From the time of the Dutch Wars a century before, the accepted way to fight with fleets at sea was 'in line of battle'. This was the logical way to fight with ships that had their guns placed on the broadside; you put your ships in line ahead, and sailed alongside, or on opposite courses to your enemy, exchanging salvoes. Over the course of years official *Fighting Instructions* had evolved to cover the various contingencies, and to ensure that over-timid and over-rash captains remained in the line. With a roughly equal enemy fleet the line was the obvious, and also the least risky, way of fighting. If the enemy fleet was definitely inferior and began to flee, you could signal 'General Chase', break up the line altogether and allow each of your ships to pursue the enemy.

Battles fought in line were rarely decisive, and by the latter 18th century the fighting instructions were rather too rigid. But it was beginning to dawn on some commanders that there might be a magic formula for winning sea battles——something known as 'breaking the line'. The first successful example of this was supposed to be the Saintes, but the greatest example was to come some 23 years later at Trafalgar. The idea was to cut your opponents' line into one or more pieces, then concentrate against one or more of the pieces. What was wrong with this theory as an answer to fighting in line was that it could only work if one's own fleet were superior to its opponents in numbers, efficiency and morale——and probably in luck. When you steer in towards the enemy line to cut it, he can fire at you with full broadsides; when you cannot reply, and once you have cut his line, he is at least as capable of concentrating his ships on you as you are on his. What would work against the badly demoralized and relatively inefficient French and Spanish fleets of the Napoleonic period would not work against the large and much more efficient and confident French fleets of the Revolutionary

Far left: French soldier, Soissonais Regiment. Vice-Admiral Comte d'Estaing had at his disposal large bodies of troops and sailors——4000 on the island of Conanicut, 3500 at the siege of Savannah——although ultimately the results were disappointing for the French and their American allies. Dress: coat, waistcoat, breeches and gaiters——white. Facings, cuffs and piping——plum red.

Centre: 1st Lieutenant, Royal Navy. Next in the chain of command after the captains were the Lieutenants. A ship of the line might carry as many as eight; smaller vessels, one or more. The senior, or first lieutenant, was responsible for the running of the ship. He did most of the executive work (captains sometimes spent a large part of their time at sea in their cabins). The second lieutenant was generally in charge of the gunnery. The coat was blue with white facings and cuffs with a white waistcoat, breeches and hose.

The illustration depicts a lieutenant with a speaking trumpet through which he would shout his commands.

Left: British Marine. By the end of the 17th century a regiment of sea soldiers was formed in England. The marines became a regular part of a ship's complement, with a ratio of one marine to every four sailors. They were as much an armed guard as a fighting force. Crews were often composed of tough characters, criminals and pressed men. The presence of disciplined men with their own officers served to control the seamen.

Dress: Coat red, facings, collar and cuffs buff, waistcoat and breeches white, black gaiters or leggings.

Opposite: American Marine Corps. Recruited by the first commissioned marine officer, Captain Samuel Nicholas at the Tun Tavern on the Philadelphia waterfront.

The marines of this period wore green jackets with red collars, lapels, cuffs, linings and turnbacks. Buff waistcoats and breeches. A hat with cockade completed the uniform.

Left: Ship's Cook. In the Royal Navy the cook was often a disabled pensioner from Greenwich Hospital. Diet deficiency was a great danger to the crews' health. Scurvy, caused by lack of fresh fruit and vegetables, was a constant threat to a ship's crew on long voyages. Lemon juice could be preserved and was only needed in small amounts, making it suitable for use aboard ship.

Below: Sail Maker. On naval vessels they were appointed by warrant. The sailmaker repaired damaged canvas and made new sails from spare canvas carried aboard. It was his job to keep the vessel moving. The principal tool of his craft, the needle and leather palm, is illustrated here.

Below: American Seaman. The American seaman, unlike his pressed British counterpart, signed on for the duration of the voyage, although the voyage was often lengthy as the cruises of John Paul Jones' squadrons proved. The pay when available was little better than their enemy's. Both relied on the capture of prize vessels.

Like the Royal Navy, there was little uniformity about the dress of the seaman. The revolutionary sailor wore loose fitting trousers wide bottomed and to the knee, a shirt or vest and perhaps a short waistcoat with a kerchief around the neck. The narrow brimmed hat was of straw or canvas and was often painted or tarred.

War period. Against this sort of enemy the only effective defense was a well-maintained line of battle, in which ships could support each other.

Another good or, perhaps, bad reason for keeping the line as the major battle formation was that other more complicated formations had to wait until a more flexible and reliable method of signaling the admiral's intentions had been found, or the admiral had un-usually intelligent and reliable subordinates upon whom he could rely to understand and follow his intentions. At the time of the American War, a full and flexible code of flag signals had yet to emerge. In 1776 Admiral Howe issued the first official British signal book to the ships under his command, but this only used the old inflexible and chaotic system of arbitrarily shown and arranged signals. The French had already been playing with systematic flag codes, but were not very far advanced.

Natural Hazards

There were almost as many losses in the course of the war from the normal hazards of seafaring as there were from the enemy. Very few ships were actually sunk in action. The British lost only one line of battle ship in battle, a '74 scuttled the day after the Battle of Chesapeake because of her leaks. It was difficult to sink a wooden ship, and even the old and leaky *Bonhomme Richard* remained afloat for hours after the

Below: Midshipmen joined the navy at a very early age, ten or twelve. From their ranks officers of the Royal Navy were promoted. (This did not apply to the Continental Navy; their officers came from the merchant marines.) Midshipmen were trained in navigation and seamanship. They were examined at nineteen for the post of Lieutenant. Promotion in peacetime without influence or examination success could be particularly slow; a midshipman of thirty or more was not rare. The coat was blue with white tabs on the collar, white cuffs, wasitcoat, breeches and hose.

terrible hammering she received in her epic fight with the *Serapis*. A few ships were unlucky enough to catch fire or blow up in action, one of the most spectacular examples being the bitter combat between the two frigates *Quebec* and *Surveillante*. The English *Quebec* had dismasted her opponent when she blew herself up and sank, leaving the survivors of both ships with a hard battle to get the shattered *Surveillante* back to Brest.

Many ships were lost by accidental explosion and fire, and many more were lost by shipwreck. The most spectacular example of the power of nature was the great West Indian hurricane of 1780; the British lost two ships of the line and ten smaller vessels, while eight more ships of the line and a 50-gun ship were badly damaged.

Nature was not only more effective than man at sinking ships, she was also a greater killer of seamen. Even if we ignore the men lost in shipwrecks and those who died of gangrenous wounds, the total of men lost through sickness is far higher than from any other cause. In the British Navy between the beginning of 1776 and September 1780, 1243 men died in action, while 18,541 were killed by disease. This was out of a total of 175,990 men who served in the Navy during that period. Still, the losses to desertion were even higher; 42,069 men were officially stated to have 'run' in the same period.

The biggest killers were tropical epidemic diseases like yellow fever, to which the fleets on the West Indies were very vulnerable. Epidemics occurred in home waters as well, and the ultimate failure of the allied Franco-Spanish fleet which threatened England with invasion in 1779 was due as much to an epidemic of 'ship fever' (typhus) which decimated its crews, as to any weakness of the Allies or efforts of the British. Of course scurvy was a great weakener and eventual killer of men on long voyages, and one of the major reasons why a policy of prolonged blockade was never a very good idea. Unfortunately for the sailors of the period, scurvy was only to be eliminated by medical advances that came after the war had ended.

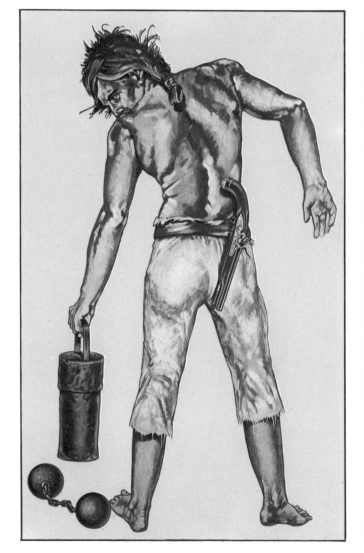

Left: Captain, Continental Navy. Probably the best known captain in the annals of American naval heroes is John Paul Jones. The fight between his ship *Bonhomme Richard* and *Serapis* is popular history, yet in the list of captains in the Continental Navy in order of seniority established by Congress, October 10th, 1776, he is only numbered 18th from a list of 24 officers holding the rank of Captain.

Dress: Coat and breeches, blue; facings, cuffs and waistcoat, red. Illustrated with a small sword.

Opposite left: British Seaman——Cannoneer. Men were taught to go about their business in silence, so that the orders of the officers and petty officers could be heard in battle. A well-trained ship's crew could clear for action and run out the guns in a very few minutes. The seaman is shown carrying a cartridge case, with chain shot at his feet.

Opposite right: Surgeon's Mate. In the ship's cockpit the surgeon and his attendants went about their gory business. Saws and knives used for amputating were warmed——a warm saw caused less agony than a cold one! A skilled man could amputate an arm at the shoulder in forty seconds. A couple of vessels were close at hand——one for washing wounds, instruments and surgeons' hands, the other for amputated limbs.

Rum, sometimes laudanum and opium, were the anesthetics; stumps were cauterized with tar and death often followed, either from shock or infection.

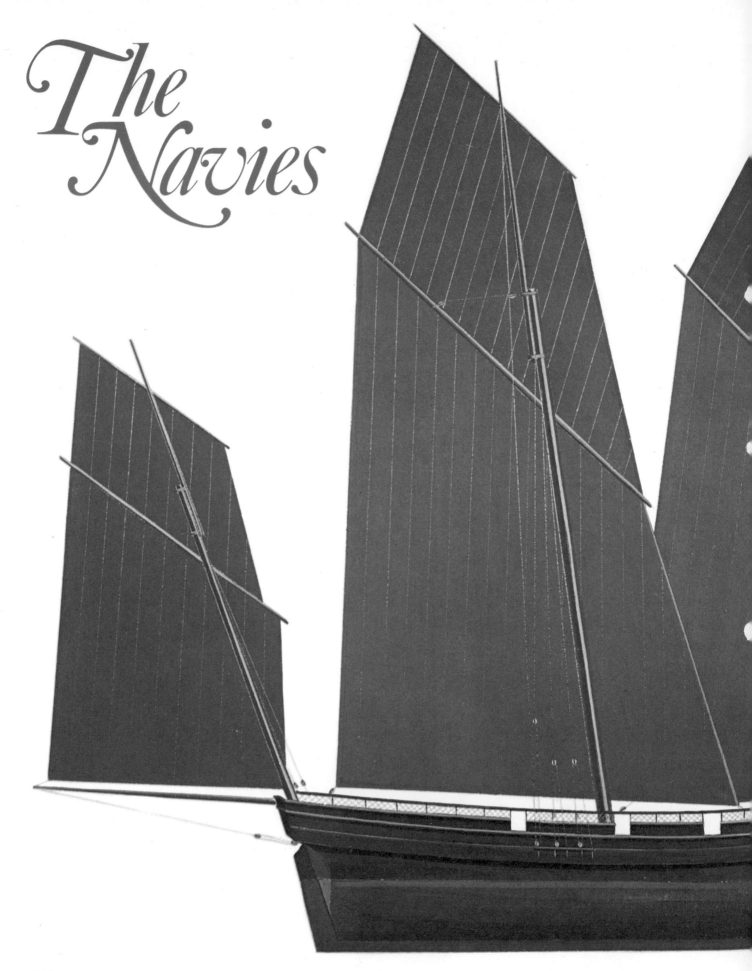

The Navies

The European Navies

It is time that we took a general look at the navies of the American War, the opponents in this great world-wide struggle, and instead of working from the biggest down we will start with the smaller navies which did not take part in the war, but whose existence could be considered to have some significance for the combatants.

We can ignore all non-European navies (except, of course, the American), but of some importance in the calculations of the diplomats on both sides were the fleets of the Scandinavian powers and of Russia. At one time, under the leadership of Russia's Catherine the Great, it seemed that the combined navies of these powers might try to prevent the British interfering with the trade in naval stores from the Baltic to the French and Spanish who relied heavily on imports of timber, cordage and the like. The League of Armed Neutrality was a diplomatic danger and was thwarted by diplomatic means. It never came to fighting, which was as well for the British, considering the number of ships controlled by the Alliance.

Of the three navies concerned——the Danish, Swedish and Russian——the Danish and the Swedish fleets had long histories, and both could call on considerable numbers of good native seamen. This was especially true of Denmark, which at this period controlled Norway. The Russian fleet, on the other hand, was a creation of the 18th century and of Czar Peter the Great, and made heavy use of officers of foreign origin like Greig to compensate for the lack of Russian nautical expertise. All three navies consisted mainly of medium-sized two-deckers generally following

Left: The lugger was as typical of small French warships as the cutter was typical of British. Like the cutter, it was developed from small coastal and fishing craft, and because of its speed and shallow draught, it was very popular among French privateers in the English Channel.

Dutch designs, which gave the shallow draught necessary for use in the Baltic.

The smallest of the three European navies which fought Britain and the last to join the struggle was the Dutch. In the previous century it had fought three bitter slogging-matches with Britain for the position of premier maritime nation in the world. The Dutch, with fewer resources and geography against them had inevitably lost, but not without an impressive garland of victories to their credit, and a glorious tradition of hard fighting and fine seamanship. There had then been a period of relative decline, when the Dutch fleet was a junior ally to the English and later a neutral. Although the Dutch still held a large overseas empire in the East Indies, South Africa and Ceylon, their fleet was now comparatively small.

However, the war proved that battles between Dutch and English ships were still bitter stand-up fights, in which the participants fought until they could fight no more. There was only one full-fledged battle between Dutch and English fleets, an affair of little tactical subtlety between two forces of two-deckers escorting convoys, which went bald-headed for one another when they met near the Dogger Bank in 1781. For four hours the two squadrons, the Dutch under Zoutman with eight ships and a total of 460 guns, against Hyde Parker's seven ships with a total of 446 guns. By the end of the battle both sides were virtually crippled. The British succeeded in getting their convoy through and the Dutch did not, and one of their ships foundered afterwards; but basically it was a drawn battle. Oddly enough, it was far and away the bloodiest action of the war, with a total of about a thousand casualties, the Dutch suffering 100 more than the British. A very high proportion of the total casualties in the naval war happened in this one action, in other ways a far smaller affair than the great fleet clashes in the Caribbean. If the revitalized French Navy had shown the same sort of dogged obstinacy as the Dutch, the final result of the war might have been different.

One of the more remarkable aspects of 18th century naval wars was the way the Spanish Navy, with an almost unbroken record of defeat, always gallantly came back for more. The ships were, as we have seen, generally well designed, though by British standards undergunned. The navy was a big one and it had large and well organized dockyards. Its chief handicap seems to have been lack of training. Officers were generally brave but in the main were not as professionally competent as their British and French contemporaries in either seamanship or tactical theory. Although Spain produced many of the best seamen in the world, her warship crews were badly disciplined, ill-trained and very badly paid and victualled. Because of this, and a general lack of decision and force in the higher direction of the war, the Spanish fleet was generally the junior partner of France in the 18th century wars, and in most of these she lost parts of her huge empire to Britain.

By far the most formidable opponent of British naval predominance was the French Navy. In the previous war it had suffered a series of crushing defeats and had ended with only a remnant of its ships. In 1758 France had only about 35 ships of the line to oppose Britain's more than 130. The very completeness of the defeat produced a desire for revenge on Britain, and there was a great naval renaissance. The church, provinces and towns gave money for the building of new ships, and a great administrator, Choiseul, built up a new and strong fleet. By 1778 France had 80 ships of the line. Since the founding of the Marine Academy at Brest in 1752, French officers were generally acknowledged to be the best educated in the theory of their profession, and French naval architects such as the great Sané had a very high reputation. As the result of the Naval Decrees of 1765, the French dockyards were now well organized, though perhaps not quite as good as the British ones in the quality of their work. French gunnery was excellent, and morale was high at the outbreak of war.

The French, however, did have certain handicaps. The power of the aristocracy meant that service rank was of less importance than in the British Navy. A junior officer of high social rank found it easier to argue with his seniors than in the British Navy, where officers' discipline was much stricter. A certain defensiveness showed itself in the favored method of firing at the enemy's rigging to cripple him. Above all the French suffered from the handicap of their orders, which were too often obsessed with the doctrine of the 'Objective', a tactical or strategic aim which was supposed to have overriding importance. Too often the Objective got in the way of achieving a decisive victory, and on many occasions in this war a French fleet which had bested an English force failed to follow up its victory because its ships were supposed to be preserved for some other purpose.

It is not surprising that the greatest French victory of the war, the Battle of the Chesapeake, was a strategic one, but tactically virtually a draw. Nor is it surprising that the one French admiral who believed in pressing on to achieving a decisive victory, the Bailli de Suffren——generally considered the greatest French sea commander of the period——never achieved a decisive success against a rather run-of-the-mill English admiral, Hughes. These two fought a series of actions off India in the closing years of the war, and it was not until the end that Suffren could get adequate support from his captains. By then it was too late, even though his last action was an unmistakeable success.

Now we come to the biggest and most successful navy of them all, the British Royal Navy. It was the oldest-established of all the major navies of the time. The French Navy had only had a continuous existence since the time of Louis XIV, a century before; the Spanish Navy had to be virtually re-created after the War of Spanish Succession; and the Dutch dated from the early years of the 17th century. But the British fleet had enjoyed a continuous, institutionalized existence since the time of Henry VII, and the previous century had been one of glorious victories. The Dutch had been subdued and the French and Spanish soundly beaten in several wars. The last conflict, the Seven Years War, had ended in over-

whelming triumph. The American War was the nearest that the British Navy came in the 18th century to outright defeat.

The British did have other advantages. Their officer corps was the most professional in the world; it might not be as well educated in theory as the French, but it had more practical experience and was better disciplined. Britain had the biggest merchant fleet, the largest reservoir of trained seamen, and the best shipyards in the world. As we have seen the Royal Dockyards were efficient ship-repairing organizations, and, though British naval architecture may have lacked some of the gloss of the French, the British excelled in making practical improvements, as the history of the carronade and of the introduction of coppering show.

The American Navies

In the years before Bunker Hill, the shipping, seamen and shipbuilding facilities of the more northerly of the Thirteen Colonies had been considered an important part of British mercantile strength. The availability of cheap timber in New England meant that in 1774 about one-third of British merchant ships were built in North America and American shipyards had already built a few warships for the British Navy. These were, admittedly, mostly smaller and less durable vessels than those built in Britain (the *average* American ship was only a 75-tonner). New England ships sailed far afield, and the American seaman was already known as a proficient and enterprising breed. When war came there was, therefore, a useful infrastructure of maritime skill and knowledge, of trained and capable seamen and of shipyards and shipbuilders.

The years of resistance to British commercial regulations which led up to the Revolution put a high premium on the building of fast, weatherly ships which could evade revenue cruisers, and the developing of the seamanlike skills to sail them. Already in the wars with France American privateers with British 'Letters of Marque' and 'Letters of Reprisal'

had established a reputation of successful ventures in private-enterprise sea-fighting. The foundations of a powerful commerce-raiding fleet had already been laid.

The American naval effort during the war took place on three different levels. First were the privateers, then the navies of the individual states, and finally the national navy organized by the Continental Congress. The privateers were by far the most successful of the three main types of American naval operations.

Almost as the first shots were being fired at Lexington, enterprising patriot merchants were beginning to arm ships to attack British transports, and soon both Congress and the various states were issuing Letters of Marque in large numbers. So many seamen and shipwrights became involved in the lucrative business of manning and building privateers that it was difficult to obtain the necessary labor and crews for setting up more regular naval forces. Even when these were set up, their major task and most successful assignment was, like the privateers, commerce raiding. In 1776 there were some 136 American privateers operating; by 1781 the number had risen to 449. The average number of guns carried rose from under ten to over fifteen. In all, privateers captured some 600 British vessels.

The earliest events in American naval history are the result of local initiative. For example, the inhabitants of the seaport of Machias in Maine captured a British armed schooner, and General Washington created his own small fleet of four army-manned ships to raid British communications. It was not long before the States and Congress began to react, however. Though all the States which created their own navies used some of their ships for some of the time in commerce-raiding ventures, their main concern tended to be with coastal defense against British bombardments and landings. Therefore most of the craft built or converted were small gunboats, galleys, or floating batteries. Only the biggest State navy, that of Massachusetts, had more seagoing ships than

Below: Old wooden ships were often kept in service long after they became unfit to go to sea. HMS *Jersey*, a 60-gun ship built in 1736, was fitted as a hospital ship in 1771. She was sent to America at the beginning of the Revolutionary War. She was also employed as a prison for captured colonists and gained notoriety for the sufferings of her captives when she was stationed near New York. The gunports were sealed down and small air and light holes were cut in each. This was done to prevent escapes, but several men did manage to escape through these 9-inch holes.

inshore craft, and the next biggest, Virginia's, only employed a very few ships in privateering. The coastal defense craft never proved to be of much use, but privateering generally paid off.

In contrast to the success of the privateers, the Continental Navy accomplished very little. In October 1775 Congress purchased two armed ships, six brigs, three schooners and five 'sloops' (of the American kind, equivalent to the British cutter) and set up a Naval Committee. The sensible decision was taken to concentrate on building powerful commerce raiders, and 13 frigates were ordered (five 32s, five 28s and three 24s). Unfortunately it is difficult to construct a disciplined and organized service quickly, and this is particularly true if there is no officer corps. Naturally enough in the circumstances, the officers were political appointees, and inevitably the majority was not particularly good at their job. Too many of the best leaders and most competent seamen preferred to join privateers. All except four of the initial program of frigates were completed, but they failed to justify the promise of their design. Most were captured or scuttled early in their careers.

In 1776, when the British Navy was still having difficulty in coping with the new war and reinforce-ments were slow in arriving, American commerce raiders were having a field day. A new building program for the Continental Navy was started. This was ambitious, including three 74s, five 36-gun frigates, and several smaller vessels. Few of these were completed, several of the part-completed hulls were in areas captured by the British. Only two of the frigates were put into service. One of these was the *Alliance*, the only major American warship to survive the war still in service with her original owners. The most successful ship of the program was John Paul Jones' famous sloop *Ranger*, which raided the English coast and captured the 20-gun British sloop *Drake*. In trying to build 74s American shipbuilders were pushing their ability and resources too far. Only one, the *America*, was completed, and then not until 1782. She was almost immediately given as a present to the French, who did not regard her very highly, and scrapped her shortly afterwards.

As the war went on the Continental Navy declined in numbers and efficiency. In 1776 it had a total of 27 vessels and about 3000 men. By early 1779, despite new ships built and purchased, there were only thirteen left. In that year a more cumbersome and less effective Board of Admiralty replaced the earlier

Left: The USS *Ranger* and HMS *Drake* after the British sloop struck. The battle took place in the Irish Sea on 24 April 1778. The *Ranger,* under the command of John Paul Jones, captured *Drake.*

Naval Committee, and by the end of the year only had nine ships to look after. By 1781 there were only three, and in that year all except one were lost.

Meanwhile other sources of ships had been tapped. In 1777 several ships were obtained in neutral but friendly France, including two frigates, though there was difficulty in delivering them, and they did not achieve much. By devious means a cutter was bought from an English shipbuilder, but diplomatic pressure forced the French (she was fitting out in one of their ports) to hand her over to the British. In 1779 an entire squadron of vessels was obtained from the French, including an old and dilapidated East Indiaman called the *Duc De Duras,* better known under her new name, *Bonhomme Richard.* Later the survivors of this squadron, together with the captured *Serapis,* were restored to the French, though other French-built vessels, including another frigate, were acquired afterwards.

Like the Continental Navy, the States' navies were reduced by capture, scuttling, and by lack of funds. Most of the ships of the Virginia Navy were lost during the 1781 raid on that state led by Benedict Arnold. In 1779 a large mixed force of ships from the Continental, Massachusetts and New Hampshire Navies, supplemented by a number of privateers, made an attack on a British outpost in Penobscot Bay. They were trapped there by a British force, which included a '64. Despite the fact that the Americans had superiority in numbers of men, ships and guns they made no real effort to fight, but instead abandoned their ships in a panic. This depressing episode shows both the moral effect of the presence of a line of battleship. There was little chance for it to prove the superiority of a larger ship against numbers of smaller ones in action, and that the Americans had not yet the organization, or the proper openings on this occasion, to indulge in regular warfare. In this war their *forte* was commerce raiding and individual actions between small ships. As an example we can take the action between the biggest vessel of the Massachusetts Navy, the 26- (or 28-) gun *Protector,*

Below: The gundalow *Loyal Convert*. This double-ended, flat-bottomed craft was one of a number built on the St. Lawrence River by the Americans in the winter of 1775–76 after their attack on Quebec. Originally named *Convert*, she was captured by the British when the Northern Army retreated, and she was renamed *Loyal Convert*. She was armed with seven 9-pdr. guns and was the forerunner of Benedict Arnold's gondolas on Lake Champlain.

which fought for an hour and a half with the large 32-gun privateer *Admiral Duff*. At the end of this time the British vessel caught fire accidentally and blew up. The success of American privateers is demonstrated by the fact that in one year (1779) there were 184 separate actions in prize courts——each one involving a captured ship——in the Commonwealth of Massachusetts alone.

Though the privateers continued to the end of the war taking British prizes, America's naval efforts had otherwise nearly petered out. The last remaining ship of the Continental Navy was sold in 1785, and for some years the new Republic had no navy at all. In material things, therefore, the war was a false start as far as the American Navy was concerned. However there had been enough successes; the cruise of the *Ranger*, the capture of the *Serapis* and the 50 or more prizes taken by the Continental Navy in 1779 (its best year), would be remembered when the failures and the losses were forgotten. Here was the foundation of the tradition of a great navy, which could say like its first great hero, 'I have not yet begun to fight'.

The ultimate administrative failure to keep a regular navy going is hardly discreditable. The new nation had to work out ways of governing itself and fight a desperate land war for its very survival, so there was little energy or material left over for the tremendously complicated task of constructing a navy. Navies were, as we have seen, very complicated and expensive forces, and took both time and special knowledge to set up, neither of which commodities the patriots had in adequate quantity. One of the worst problems was the finding of guns for the ships. There was a not very successful attempt to set up cannon foundries in America during the war, but Congress mainly had to rely on captured British weapons, and whatever could be smuggled in from Europe. Gunpowder was in equally short supply and, as with crews, it was the privateers who had the money and obtained the first choice. As a result most ships went to sea with 'job lots' of cannon of varying.sizes, types and ages. The *Bonhomme Richard*'s 18-pounders

which were so old and poor that they exploded in action are a good example of what the officers of the new navy had to put up with.

As we have seen, during the early years of the war, when only Britain and America were adversaries, there was hardly any possibility of major single-ship actions, let alone big fleet actions. The Americans had almost no ships of significant size, and those that they finally did manage to build had an almost uniform lack of success. Yet American naval activity was not unimportant in the strategic sense. The privateers and the smaller navy ships did manage to tie down large numbers of British warships and, both from captures and from the French via St. Eustacius in the West Indies, to keep a steady stream of useful items——guns, powder, money, and even uniforms ——flowing to Washington's hard-pressed army. Equally important, they caused considerable disruption in Britain's supply lines at sea.

Perhaps the most strategically important action fought by American naval forces in the early years neither occurred at sea nor was it a tactical victory. Yet it comes close to deserving the soubriquet 'decisive'.

In the winter of 1775 a daring American attack on Canada had nearly succeeded, but the arrival of British reinforcements led to a retreat which came perilously near to a rout. The shattered American troops were withdrawn down Lake Champlain, the best invasion route from Canada to New York, and obviously the way a British army would attack. The task of defending the lake was given to one of the leaders of the earlier attack on Canada, Benedict Arnold. He immediately set about building a fleet to sail on the lake and prevent the British from advancing until they had built their own fleet. The British had the advantages: trained seamen, better supplies, more support from home. But building a fleet in the wilderness took time; it was not until late in 1776 that a superior British fleet sailed against Arnold.

The American leader chose for his schooners, gundalows and galleys, a concealed position between

Valcour Island and the shore line. It was not until the British sailed past this position, on their way south along the narrow lake, that they saw the Americans. This meant that the British vessels had to beat back against the wind, and their most powerful ships, the radeau *Thunderer* and a ship-rigged sloop, never got into action at all. The first British schooner to reach the American line was badly mauled, and was only saved by the heroic efforts of a tall teenager, Edward Pellew, later to win fame as an outstanding frigate captain and then as an Admiral, Viscount Exmouth. However, as the British gunboats rowed into position, and the other ships came up, the superior weight of British fire began to tell. With some vessels hopelessly damaged, Arnold could fight no more, and after nightfall the surviving ships managed to escape, only to be scuttled at the southern end of the lake as the British advanced.

Arnold had known that all he could do, once the British had built their fleet, was to fight a gallant and hopeless delaying action with his hastily built ships and his part-trained soldier crews. He had the satisfaction of knowing that his real aim was already secure. It was too late in the year for the British to advance further, and time was the most vital need if the new nation was to survive. Valcour Island was a glorious defeat for American arms, and its consequence the following year was Burgoyne's defeat at Saratoga——one of the most important American victories of the war, since it impelled France to come in on the American side.

Because the British were usually the victors in small seafights, the rare occasions in which they lost tended to take on a particular psychological value to their enemies. It is primarily for this reason that the duel between the *Bonhomme Richard* and the *Serapis* has become one of the most famous naval battles of all time.

John Paul Jones had already distinguished himself when, as Captain of the sloop *Ranger* in 1777, he had made a series of daring raids on the English coast and had captured the British sloop *Drake*. The British anathematized him as a pirate; the Americans and French celebrated him as a hero; and in the process, his exploits had gained in importance out of all proportion to their military value.

Thus the stage was already set for drama when, in 1779, Jones, leading a small squadron, put to sea in the converted French Indiaman *Bonhomme Richard* in search of a fat British convoy. He found it on 25 September, off the Yorkshire coast near Flamborough Head.

It was a Baltic convoy, escorted by the 44-gun ship *Serapis* and a sloop. On sighting the superior American squadron the two British ships immediately took the correct action in the circumstances, placing themselves between the convoy and the enemy. The accounts of the battle that follow vary in their details; and it is difficult to know whether to give more reliance to that of Pierson, the British captain, who was naturally enough making excuses for his defeat, or of Jones, who was apt to exaggerate his own achievements.

But the broad outline of the fight between the two big ships is clear enough. After each tried to rake the other, and after a couple of near-collisions when each ship in turn got entangled with her opponent's bowsprit, they fell alongside and battered away at each other for two hours by moonlight. The *Serapis* had the advantage in gunpower, and though her guns were, like the American ship's, old, they did not burst. She eventually silenced the *Richard*'s lower deck battery, but the French marines and the seamen in the tops of the *Richard* had effectively cleared the *Serapis*' upper deck by their superior firepower, and hand grenades had set the British ship on fire in several places. This stalemate was finally ended by two things. One was a well-aimed hand grenade which exploded some cartridges on board *Serapis*, causing casualties and confusion, but even this would not have been enough. The decisive weapon was the superior willpower and nerve of Jones, who kept his crew fighting, and finally secured the British ship's surrender despite the fact that his own ship was sinking under him.

Meanwhile, what was happening to the other ships during this desperate struggle? The British sloop had been dismasted and surrendered to one of the two frigates in Jones' squadron. The other frigate was commanded by a very odd Frenchman, who fired a few ill-aimed shots during this lesser battle, and then sailed round the two bigger ships, firing a number of salvoes which, Jones claimed, hit the *Richard,* and missed the *Serapis* altogether. Whether this is true or not, it is certain that Jones got remarkable little support during his action against a ship that was about the same nominal power as his own, but was actually superior by virtue of being a new purpose-built warship. The other Franco-American ships had failed to catch the convoy, so the British warships had succeeded in their basic purpose, but this does not diminish the stature of Jones' victory——a rare example of sheer force of personality triumphing over material inferiority——nor the tremendous effect his success had on the morale of the allies.

A similar example of a small seafight that had disproportionate consequences had occurred a few years earlier, on the eve of the French entry into the war. The handy little French frigate *Belle Poule* (30 guns), under the command of the scion of a famous naval family, Isaac de la Clocheterie, put to sea in June, 1778. Accompanied by another small frigate and a lugger, de la Clocheterie was cruising up the English Channel when he sighted a British fleet of twenty sail under the command of Admiral Keppel.

France and England were still technically at peace, but relations were strained to the breaking point and hostilities were implicit in every encounter. Several of the faster British ships instantly detached themselves from Keppel's squadron and set out in pursuit of the French. *Arethusa,* a 32-gun frigate said to be the fastest in the Royal Navy, along with the cutter *Alert,* soon overhauled *Belle Poule* and the lugger (the other French frigate had fled in panic). Words were exchanged, insults followed, and soon the four ships were exchanging brisk cannon fire.

The fight lasted for five hours. *Alert* made off with the hapless lugger, but the two frigates were locked in bitter, even-handed combat. De la Clocheterie stubbornly refused to disengage, and in the end it was the *Arethusa* that turned tail and ran back to the protection of Keppel's squadron. After firing a few contemptuous parting shots, the battered *Belle Poule* triumphantly set her sails for France.

Nothing of military importance had been decided, but the news of de la Clocheterie's little triumph was received in France with something akin to delirium. Proud of its new naval strength, frantic for revenge against the hated English and already deep in the grip of war fever, the French were jubilant over this humiliation of their ancient enemy. De la Clocheterie was personally decorated by the King and fashionable court ladies began to wear their hair à la *Belle Poule,* a huge pompadour surmounted, incredibly, by a model of a full-rigged frigate.

It is not possible to say with precision what the *Belle Poule* vs. *Arethusa* incident——following as it did on the heels of the news of Saratoga and the successful diplomacy of Ben Franklin——may have contributed to hastening France into the war with Britain. But even to have added a little to France's resolve to fight was a considerable accomplishment for so small a ship.

No such acclaim attended the multifarious, but vitally important activities of the American privateers. Indeed, no individual action involving a privateer could even be said to be typical, but perhaps the story of Captain Haraden may be cited as representative. Late in 1779, Jonathan Haraden, equipped with a letter-of-marque, sailed the *General Pickering,* a small 16-gun ship, out of Salem, Massachusetts, on a raiding cruise. Off Bilbao, Spain, Haraden ran afoul of the 22-gun British privateer *Golden Eagle,* which he contrived to capture without firing a shot. The following day, Haraden was pursued by a large 42-gun British privateer, but by a combination of skillful maneuvering and determined fighting, he drove her off. When he finally landed at Bilbao, the local Spanish citizenry treated him as a hero. On the return voyage Haraden captured three British merchantmen,

Below: The surrender of Cornwallis at Yorktown, by John Trumbull. Despite the fact that the Battle of the Virginia Capes was not a clear-cut French victory, it was sufficient to prevent Cornwallis' escape from the encirclement of the armies of Washington, Rochambeau and Lafayette. His surrender made a negotiated peace with the Americans inevitable. Although the Battle of the Saintes in 1782 was a major British victory and the greatest sea battle of the war, it came too late to save America for Britain. American independence was insured on the field at Yorktown and on the waters of the Chesapeake.

two armed with fourteen guns and the other with twelve. Haraden made several other successful cruises and ended the war a rich man. The total value of his captures is indicated by the fact that they contributed something in excess of 1000 guns to the American cause.

Naval engagements of fleet size did not take place until after France and her allies had entered the war on the American side. Such big actions as did then occur tended either to be tactically uninteresting and strategically important or just the other way round. There were no Trafalgars or Midways in this war, but there were some important battles, nonetheless.

The first major battle between fleets took place in the Atlantic off Ushant on 27 July 1778. The French, under d'Orvilliers, had 32 ships of the line, while Keppel, the British Admiral, had 30. The two fleets had been in sight of one another for four days, and there had been much preliminary maneuvering, with the French retaining the 'weather gauge'. This meant that they stayed to windward of the British fleet, giving themselves the choice of engaging or avoiding action at will. However, on the morning of 27th, the direction of the wind changed, Keppel was able to cross his opponent's wake, and sail up towards the French rear. To save his hindmost ships being engaged one by one, d'Orvilliers turned all the ships in his fleet round and sent them back the way they came. Both the fleets were sailing as close into the wind as they could, the French wanting to keep at long range, the British, to close with them. They passed each other firing as they went; the first few French ships were out of range, but the rest did much damage to the British fleet's masts and rigging. Keppel tried to engage again, but the disabling of several of his ships, and a communications failure between him and his second in command, prevented this.

The French had suffered more casualties (163 killed and 573 wounded, against the British total of 133 killed and 375 wounded), but they had done far more damage to their opponent's ships. Yet instead of following up this advantage, d'Orvilliers took advan-

tage of his superior mobility to return to Brest. This set a general pattern for the battles of the war, the French winning tactical advantages against slightly smaller British fleets, but failing to follow them up fully. Unfortunately for the British, the failure of communications between commander and deputy was inflamed for political reasons into a first class row which led to court martial for both, and the resignation of one and the removal of the other from com-

mand at sea. Command of the Channel Fleet subsequently went to an aged and, unsuitable admiral whose record in the next year was dismal.

After the Battle of Ushant there were no more major fleet engagements between British and French in European waters, though there were a number of minor encounters. In the West Indies and American waters, however, the situation was different, and here there were numerous battles between British and French fleets, usually either equal in strength, or with a slight numerical superiority on the French side. On the occasions when the French succeeded in disabling British ships, they often repeated their error at Ushant in failing to pursue the advantage. The British, on the other hand, never managed to catch the French at enough of a disadvantage to win a complete victory until 1782.

Soon after their entry into the war, the French began sending fleets of warships across the Atlantic. The first to reach American waters in 1778 comprised some eleven ships of the line, plus various smaller warships and transports. By August, it had fallen foul of Admiral Howe's New York squadron and had fought a sprawling inconclusive battle off Rhode Island that seems to have convinced both French Admiral d'Estaing, and apparently, Howe as well, that nothing much was to be gained by repeating the engagement. D'Estaing subsequently sailed south to the Caribbean, where he harried British naval and land forces, and then went home.

The second French fleet arrived in 1780, bringing seven ships of the line to North America and depositing General Rochambeau and his troops, come to aid Washington, ashore on Rhode Island without incident. In March 1781 this fleet, too, fought an indecisive action with the British. The French, under the command of Admiral Destouches, had wanted to bring aid to Lafayette in his campaign against Benedict Arnold (now fighting for the British) in the Chesapeake area. But the French squadron was intercepted by an approximately equal force of British ships under the command of Admiral Arbuthnot, and though the ensuing fight was again inconclusive, the French could not break through to the Chesapeake, and so had to abandon their objective and return to their base at Newport. In recognition of their non-achievement, both Destouches and Arbuthnot were replaced by their respective Admiralties.

Unlike its predecessors, the third French fleet to appear on the American scene was to play a rôle that was decisive. This was the main French fleet that had been operating against the British for several years in the West Indies. In August 1781, at the urging of Washington and Rochambeau, it sailed north with 28 ships of the line. Its object was twofold: to make possible, via sea transport, the concentration of American forces about the besieged city of Yorktown, and to prevent the British navy from coming to the relief of the British troops in Yorktown.

Below: The Maltese galley is a representative of the galleys used by Spain. These craft descended from the great war-galleys of medieval times, and although useless for ocean warfare, these galleys could nip out and catch an enemy warship becalmed in the Mediterranean off the Spanish coast.
Overleaf: Closing stage of the Battle of the Saintes. In this last major sea battle of the war, and the biggest battle, the British destroyed the French fleet in the West Indies. Since negotiations for peace with the Americans were already well underway, the British made considerable capital out of this victory in their effort to retain most of their empire from the French and Spanish, who were seeking to regain some of the losses they suffered at British hands during the Seven Years War.

Upon arriving at the Chesapeake, the French admiral, de Grasse, immediately set up his blockade. The British fleet, as it was bound to do, attacked as quickly as possible. On 5 September, in what is known as the Battle of the Virginia Capes (or the Chesapeake), the British failed to break through the French line. Before the British could regroup for a second assault, de Grasse was reinforced by the arrival of the French squadron from Newport. Now the French, with a total of 36 ships of the line, had such a local preponderance of power that the British could not hope to dislodge them. The doom of Cornwallis and British troops at Yorktown had been sealed.

With fatal inevitability, the Americans closed the ring. Washington's troops were brought by sea to Williamsburg and then march overland to Yorktown. Cornwallis, cut off by land and by sea, held out only until 19 October. His surrender broke the will of Britain to continue the war in America. Many things had gone into the winning of American independence, the French Navy was not the least of them.

With the conclusion of the fighting in America, the original and principal cause of the war had been removed. Yet it was not possible to bring hostilities being conducted all over the globe to an immediate conclusion. Curiously, in the interval between the surrender at Yorktown and the time the news of the Treaty of Paris had reached all the scattered combatants, some of the most brilliant naval campaigns of the war were fought.

One took place so far from either Europe or America that it seems almost to have been part of another war. In 1781 the man who was to prove the ablest of all French naval commanders, the Bailli de Suffren, set sail from Brest with a small squadron to give aid to the Dutch on the Cape of Good Hope, who were expecting a British attack. The Dutch fears were well founded, for on 16 April, de Suffren intercepted the anticipated British naval expedition and gave them a thrashing that effectively put a stop to their mission.

American Naval Flags and Pennants.
Top left: This flag flew on the American ship *Alliance* in 1779.
Top right: The flag flown in 1779 on the *Serapis*, the prize ship taken by John Paul Jones from the British during the most hard fought naval engagement of the entire Revolutionary War.
(Illustrations based on sketches made by a Dutch artist on the island of Texel, Holland. The originals may be seen in the Gunther Collection of the Chicago Historical Society.)
Bottom: Two American naval pennants based on the Mondhare flagsheet of 1781. The top pennant with cantons and stars appears to have at least three or more vertical stripes. The lower pennant is without canton or stars.

Strength of The British Navy

Type	End of war 1763	Before start of war 1775	End of war 1783
100 guns	5	4	5
98-90 guns	15	16	19
84 guns	1	1	1
80 guns	7	3	4
76 guns	—	—	1
74 guns	37	57	81
70 guns	11	7	4
68-66 guns	3	—	2
64 guns	30	32	49
60 guns	32	11	8
Total line of battle ships	141*	131	174*
56 guns	—	—	2
52 guns	—	—	1
50 guns	24	12	20
44 guns	21	4	28
40 guns Frigates	—	—	2
38 guns Frigates	2	—	7
36 guns Frigates	4	3	17
34 guns Frigates	—	—	1
32 guns Frigates	32	35	59
30 guns Frigates	2	—	1
28 guns Frigates	22	24	33
26 guns Frigates	—	—	1
24 guns Frigates	22	7	11
22 + 20	13	13	15
Sloops, 18-8	57	38	85
Bombs	14	2	4
Fireships	11	1	17
General total	365	270	468

*These totals do not include some foreign prizes, captured, but not yet purchased for British use (7 in 1763, 4 in 1783). The figures do not include non-operational craft like yachts, dockyard vessels and hulks.

French, Spanish, Dutch and American Warship Losses 1777-1783

Types	French	Spanish	Dutch	American	Total
104s	1	—	—	—	1
80s	—	1	—	—	1
74s	9	—	—	—	9
70s	—	7	—	—	7
64s	6	—	1	—	7
60s	—	—	1	—	1
54s	—	—	1	—	1
50s	—	—	1	—	1
44s	—	—	—	1	1
40s & 38s	4	—	1	2	7
36s & 32s	17	2	1	6	26
30s & 28s	2	3	1	7	13
Corvettes/ post ships	7	1	—	6	14
sloops & smaller	20	—	2	17	39
Armed ships	2	—	—	—	2
Floating batteries	—	10	—	—	10
Flutes (transport conversions of warships)	4	—	—	—	4
Total	72	24	9	39	144

The American total includes ships lost from the various states' navies as well as the navy organized by Congress.

Of the above totals four of the French 74s, one of their 64s, one of their 40s and an armed ship were lost through accident or stress of weather. Two of the American sloops foundered; otherwise all the ships enumerated here were lost in action against the British Navy. Probably in all four navies more ships were lost at sea than are included here, and the totals for the action losses among the smaller vessels are almost certainly too low. The American totals do not include lake and river craft.

British, French, Spanish and Dutch Line of Battle Ships Known To Have Served in The War

Types (guns)	French	Spanish	Dutch	Allied total	British
1st Rates	6	2	—	8	3
98 & 90	—	—	—	—	13
86 & 84	2	2	—	4	1
80	7	7	—	14	3
76	—	—	1	1	—
74	48	1	4	53	57
70 & 68	—	48	5	53	2
64	27	11	9	47	34
60	—	4	5	9	5
56 & 54	—	—	12	12	—
50	10	2	6	18	17
Total	100	77	42	219	135

These are effective totals, of ships which were in a fit state to go to sea. This explains why the British figures are somewhat less than those given in the table of British strength, which includes ships used as hulks and for harbor service of other kinds. The figures given are a cumulative total for the entire war, and include vessels lost to the enemy and the elements. In the case of ships taken by one power from another these are only counted under the original owner. There are, however, a few French (one 80, three 74s and one 64) and one Spanish (a 74) ships captured by the British in the previous war counted in the British total. Although 50s were generally considered as too small to lie in the line of battle they still did so in the course of this war. The considerable number of British 44s are not counted, however.

The Navies of The Armed Neutrality

Type	Denmark	Sweden	Russia	Total
94	—	1	—	1
90	—	1	—	1
76	—	—	3	3
74	1	—	—	1
70	5	6	—	11
66	—	1	9	10
64	3	—	7	10
60	3	5	—	8
50	2	—	3	5
46	1	—	—	1
42 & 40	1	2	3	6
38, 36 & 34	6	6	1	13
32s	1	4	4	9
30 & 28	1	2	—	3
26 & 24 & 20	1	—	4	5
Total	25	28	34	87

This list does not include smaller craft such as galleys, gunboats and the like owned in some numbers by these navies.

British Navy Losses 1775-1783

Type	*Captured*	*Lost in action*	*Total lost in action and captured*	*Wrecks etc.*	*Total*
1st & 2nd rates	—	—	—	2	2
74s & 70s	—	1	1	7 + 2	10
64s	1	—	1	3	4
50s	2	—	2	2	4
44s	3	1	4	1	5
36s	1	—	1	2	3
32s	5	5	10	6	16
28s	4	4	8	7	15
Post ships	6	3	9	10	19
Sloops	42	5	47	26	73
Armed ships	5	1	6	6	12
Transports, etc.	2	—	2	3	5
Brigs, cutters, schooners, etc.	18	2	20	9	29
Fireships & bombs	1	1	2	4	6
Total	90	23	113	88 + 2	203

Quite a few of the *captured* vessels were later recaptured by the British Navy, including the one captured 64, one 44, two 32s, three port ships, eight sloops and two cutters. These recaptured have not been taken away from the total of losses to enable a closer comparison to be made with the tables of French, and other losses, in which these ships are also shown. The vast majority of the captured ships shown here were taken by the French.

Most of the ships shown as *lost in action* were scuttled when in danger of capture, like the frigates sunk as block ships when the French fleet appeared off Rhode Island in 1778. Only a few blew up or caught fire in action, or sank as a result of damage sustained in battle, like the single 74 (which was finally scuttled because she leaked too much after the Battle of the Chesapeake).

The *wrecks* column includes ships lost by stranding, foundering, accidental explosions, or fires. The entry for 74s includes two ships of this class which were broken up in the West Indies as being too worn for further service (this explains the '+ 2', they were not true losses, as they would have been broken up earlier if it had been peacetime).

This list does not include some of the smallest vessels, nor does it include those ships which fought on Lake Champlain.

Warship Prizes Taken into British Service 1777-1783

Types	*French*	*Spanish*	*Dutch*	*American*	*Total*
1st rate	1	—	—	—	1
3rd rates	7	5	—	—	12
Small two-deckers	—	—	3	—	3
Frigates	16	4	2	4	26
Post ships	3	—	—	3	6
Sloops & armed ships	6	—	—	3	9
Total	33	9	5	10	57

This list does not include many smaller craft, or captured privateers, several of which were taken into the British Navy. Nor does it take in the river and lake craft used during the war in America.

Typical Warships of The Revolutionary War, Dimensions & Tonnage

Type	*Length* *feet*	*inches*	*Breadth* *feet*	*inches*	*Depth* *feet*	*inches*	*Tons*
1st rate 104, France	185	7½	53	7½	22	2	2347
1st rate 100, Britain	178	0	51	9½	21	6	2047
2nd rate 90, Britain	177	6	50	2	21	2	1943
2nd rate 84, Britain	175	4	50	3½	20	1	1918
3rd rate 80, France (2 decks)	180	5	50	3	23	0	1977
3rd rate 80, Spain (2 decks)	178	10¾	53	3¾	22	4	2184
3rd rate 80, Britain (3 decks)	165	0	47	3	20	0	1579
3rd rate 74, Britain (on French lines, large)	171	3	49	9	21	3	1825
3rd rate 74, Britain (medium size)	168	6	47	3	18	9½	1645
3rd rate 74, France	175	0	47	4½	21	3	1718
3rd rate, 70, Spain	170	2¼	51	2¼	22	1¼	1926
3rd rate 64, Britain	160	2	44	5	18	11	1383
4th rate 62, Holland	143	8¾	41	8½	16	0	1075
4th rate 50, Britain	146	1	40	8	17	6	1053
5th rate 44, Britain	140	0	37	10	16	4	886
Frigate, 40, France	158	8	40	4	13	6	1153
Frigate, 38, Britain	141	0	38	10	13	9	941
Frigate, 36, France	140	0	37	10	11	11	903
Frigate, 36, Spain	144	10	38	8	11	7¼	951
Frigate, 32, Britain	126	0	35	7	12	2	697
Frigate, 32, France	133	5	36	8	11	0	782
Frigate, 32, America[1]	159	9	37	0	12	3	970
Frigate, 28, Britain	120	6	33	9	11	0	603
24, Britain	114	3	32	0	10	3	514
20, Britain	108	6	30	1	9	8	432
Ship sloop 18, France	94	11	27	6½	14	4¼	305
Ship sloop 16, Britain	98	1	27	4	13	4	318
Brig sloop 14, Britain	78	10	25	3	11	6	205
Schooner, 10, America	71	6	20	6	8	0	132
Cutter, 10, Britain	65	7	24	3	9	7	152
Galley, 10, America[2]	72	4	19	7	6	2	123
Bomb, 8, Britain	91	6	27	8	12	1	302

Notes

(1) This was the *Confederacy* (*Confederate*), taken into the British Navy as a 36.

(2) The *Washington*, one of the Lake Champlain galleys.

The *length* given is the 'length on the gun deck', roughly equivalent to our length between perpendiculars. It was the basic length of the hull without counting the extra length of stem piece, bowsprit, etc. The *depth* used is 'depth in hold', roughly speaking the distance between the gun deck and the top of the frames above the keel. The *tonnage* is 'old builders' measurement', and was found by using the length, breadth and depth of the ship in a formula which gave an answer including parts of a ton measured in 94ths. These fragments are not given above to avoid complication. The resulting figure is a measure of the capacity of the hull, not of weight or displacement.

All the figures given come from ships which fell into British hands, or were British-built. This removes difficulties in comparing different national measurements (of which there were quite a few at the time) as the British measured and took the lines off most of the vessels they captured.

Below: This gunboat is typical of the type used by the British, particularly on Lake Champlain in 1776. She carried only one gun on a carriage which was inclined upwards to reduce the recoil. The gun would normally have been an 18-pdr. or 24-pdr., but the hull was only 37 feet long and three feet four inches deep.

Bottom: HMS *Atalanta*, a 14-gun sloop, which fought in the war. This is the plan from which the ship was built, and the original is housed at the National Maritime Museum, Greenwich, London, England.

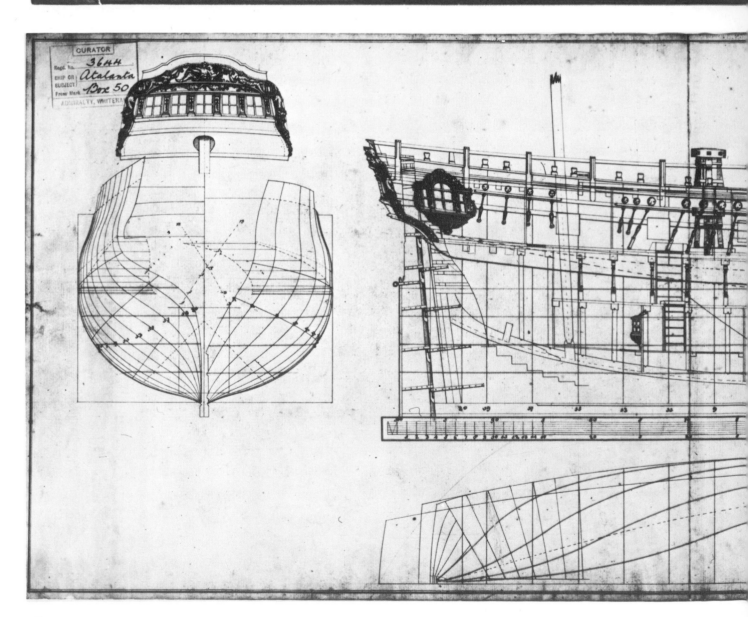

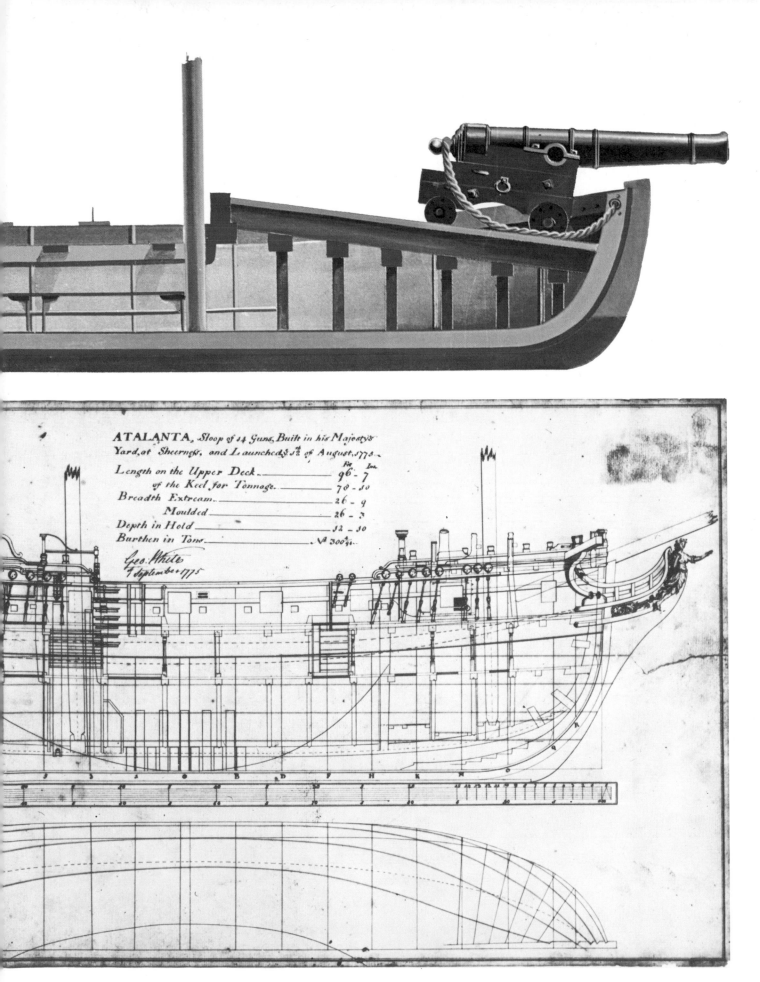

ATALANTA, Sloop of 14 Guns, Built in his Majesty's
Yard, at Sheerness, and Launched 5th of August, 1775.

	Feet	Inc
Length on the Upper Deck	96	7
of the Keel for Tonnage	78	10
Breadth Extream	26	9
Moulded	26	3
Depth in Hold	12	10
Burthen in Tons	300	94⁄

Geo. White
7 September 1775

Rounding the Cape, de Suffren sailed on into the Indian Ocean. He had no illusions about displacing the British from India, but he had a shrewd idea that if he mounted a campaign in the Bay of Bengal British efforts elsewhere could be weakened. And so he did. Furiously aggressive, he attacked the British wherever he found them. He fought five savage naval battles with the forces of the local British Admiral, Sir Edward Hughes, captured the British base at Trincomalee, Ceylon, and gave great encouragement to Hyder Ali, the Sultan of Mysore, then at war with the British in India. Despite the small size of his force

and the fact that he had no port in which to refit, de Suffren maintained his offensive continuously for a year and a half, by the end of which time he was, if anything, in a better military position than ever. The Treaty of Paris brought an abrupt end to his campaign, but he returned home a hero.

The greatest British naval action of the war also took place in the post-Yorktown limbo, and one ironic result of this action was that de Grasse, the architect of the Yorktown victory, was to become the prisoner of the same British Commander who had failed to break him off the Virginia Capes. This was

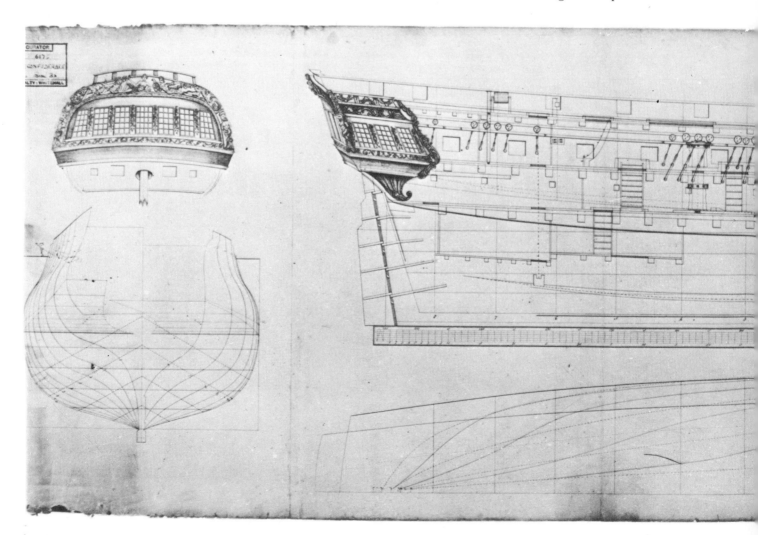

Below: The *Confederate* after her lines were taken off (measured) in 1781. Originally the USS *Confederacy*, shown on the cover of this book, she was captured by the British in 1776 and with her name altered, she was pressed into service with the Royal Navy. Every prize of war was measured by the British before being put into active service, and the plans were stored in the Admiralty. This ship was studied with special interest because of the unusual shape of her hull.

Admiral Rodney, an old and sick man who nevertheless had a good record and a reputation as an excellent tactician. In early 1782 Rodney at last had more ships than his opponent (37 as against 31), and took full advantage of this superiority at a battle fought near a small group of islands known as the Saintes on 12 April.

The French were hoping to attack Jamaica and were sailing to join the Spanish fleet for this purpose. On 8 April Rodney sighted the French fleet near Dominica. On the 9th, de Grasse, who had hoped to slip past the British and carry out his original plan, was presented with the opportunity of attacking Hood's van squadron which had become separated from the main British fleet. He only sent fifteen of his ships, and these made two attacks on Hood but were kept from closing because of their fear of British carronades. The imminent arrival of the main British body finally frightened them off.

For the next two days the French stayed out of the clutch of the British fleet, but were also kept from increasing their distance by the slow sailing of ships badly hit in the action with Hood. Towards sunset on the 11th Rodney was close enough for both fleets

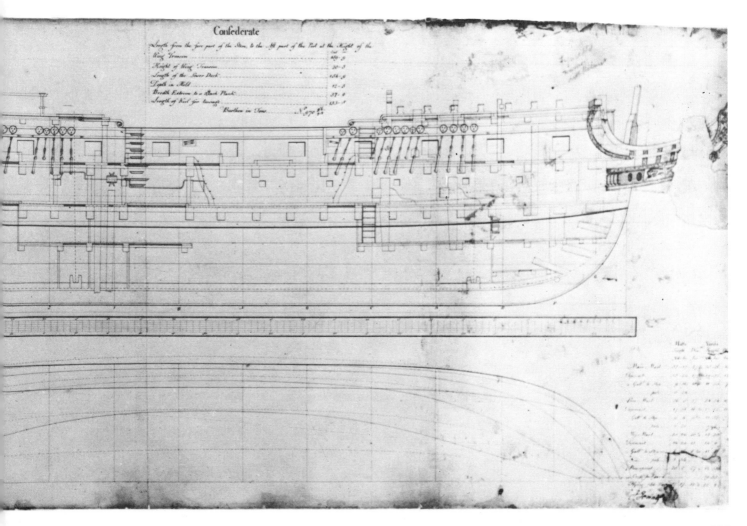

to form lines of battle, but it was too late in the day to fight.

When dawn came, the British ships saw that one French vessel had been disabled by a collision in the night. This crippled vessel was the lure which caused the two fleets to close one another. De Grasse was still trying to avoid close action, but at about 9 a.m. his luck deserted him. The French line was already in some disorder, when a sudden shift in the wind gave Rodney an opening. He immediately took his flagship, the *Formidable*, through the French line, dismantling one French ship by his broadsides in passing. Rodney's Flag Captain, Douglas, saw his gunnery

reforms produce excellent results on this day. Douglas' old ship, the *Duke*, immediately ahead of Rodney in the line, also cut through the French, inflicting much damage as she did so. The sixth ship astern of Rodney showed equal initiative on this occasion by also cutting through the French line. It was followed by the entire British rear.

The French formation was completely shattered. Those French ships that could still sail now tried to escape and most of them did so, for Rodney did not make any great effort to pursue. Hood, who just managed to catch up with and capture the damaged French flagship before nightfall, was bitterly critical

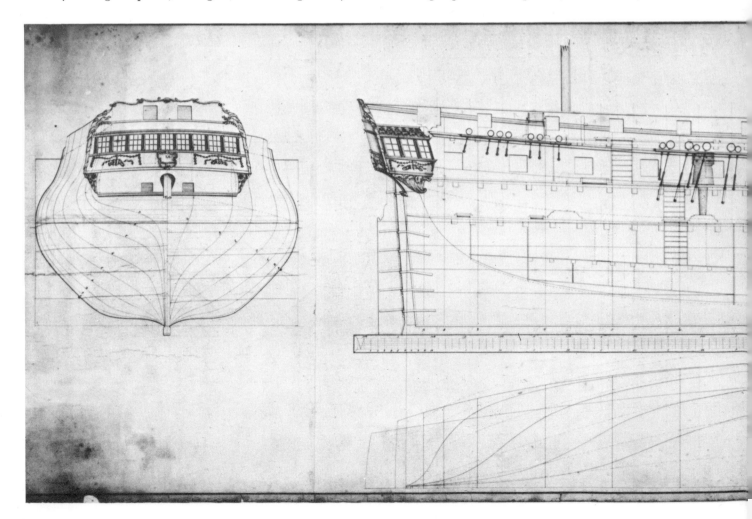

of his chief for this. However, the French fleet had often proved that it could sail faster than the British; and it was unlikely that many of the French ships could have been caught, however keen the pursuit. As Rodney himself said: 'Come, we have done very handsomely'. Five French ships and their commander-in-chief had been captured, and some days later Hood added to the French discomfiture by capturing another two line of battle ships and a couple of other vessels.

When the war ended, the balance of international naval power seemed much as before. Britain was still indisputably the premier naval power in the world. Single-handed, the British had fought the combined might of four navies to a standstill. The French were still firmly in second place. The Spanish had again demonstrated their capacity for gallant failure. The Dutch had, if nothing else, proven that the tenacious spirit of their great 17th century admirals had not disappeared. The American Navy——a new presence on the military scene——had ceased to exist.

Yet some subtle, far-reaching changes had occurred. The French had every reason to be encouraged; never before had they done so well against their ancient foe. And the British, despite their last-minute victory at the Saintes, had some cause for concern; for the most part, they had signally failed to inflict on their

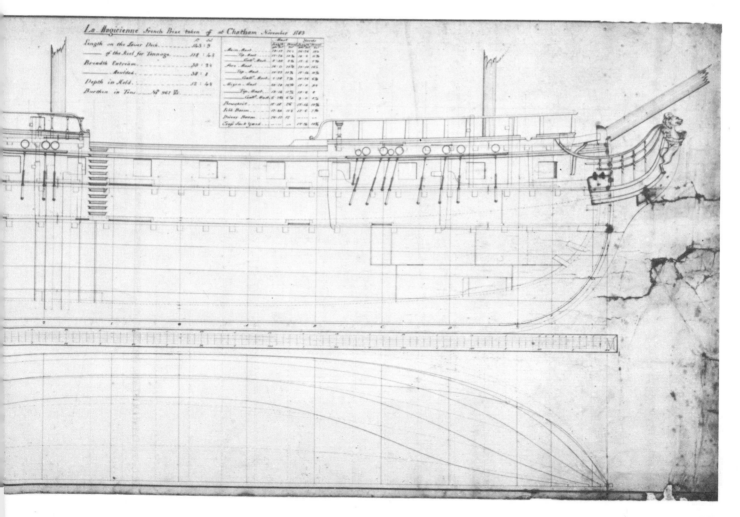

Below: The American cutter *Lee* was a specialized shallow-draught warship for use on Lake Champlain, quite unlike the normal seagoing cutter. A much more sophisticated and weatherly craft than the gundalow, *Lee* was sunk in August 1776, and was later raised and taken into the Royal Navy.
Left: Flamborough Head, from a photograph taken in 1957. The *Bonhomme Richard* and *Serapis* fought their classic battle off this point on the Yorkshire coast in 1779.

enemies the kind of crushing defeats that had formerly been the glory of the Royal Navy. In both countries young naval officers would be giving much thought to the matter of improved strategy and tactics, and the results of that thought would soon be translated into action in the great naval clashes of the wars between Britain and Revolutionary and Napoleonic France.

Perhaps the greatest apparent lesson of the war concerned the primacy of strategy over tactics in naval warfare. The French policy of pursuing the 'objective', even at the occasional expense of tactical advantage, seemed to have been vindicated. At Yorktown de Grasse had achieved a decisive local superiority in support of an extremely important strategic objective. No matter that his ships did not conduct themselves with any special brilliance against the attacking forces of Graves and Rodney; the objective was attained and a campaign was won.

To be fair, the true art of war lies not so much in dismissing tactics for the sake of strategy, or vice versa, but in achieving the greatest possible coordination between the two. Learning to master this art was something that all the navies of the world needed to do——and possibly always will.

The naval war showed that the British Navy still deserved its premier position. Despite numerical odds and domestic strife, despite occasional mismanagement and badly strained resources, it could fight a combination of every other major navy and survive. One British army was lost at Yorktown because of a naval defeat, but other, larger armies were not lost; instead for years they were fed and supported by British naval and mercantile power. British merchant ships were badly hit by French and American attacks, but by the end of the war American naval forces had dwindled nearly to nothing under British attacks, and few French merchantmen ventured out from their ports. The French Navy had given convincing proof of its excellence, but in the end the one great naval victory of the war was British.

The formal American Navy had been virtually wiped out during the course of the war. Yet——again in strategic terms——American naval activity, in all its aspects, achieved much. It had provided time and guns for Saratoga and vitally needed money and weapons for Washington's army. It had distracted many British warships from more important assignments and had inflicted serious harm on the British merchant marine. Most important, perhaps, it had established the foundations——the experience, the personnel and the tradition——for the eventual creation of a permanent navy that would one day become the greatest on earth.

By the KING.

A PROCLAMATION,

Declaring the Ceſſation of Arms, as well by Sea as Land, agreed upon between His Majeſty, the Moſt Chriſtian King, the King of *Spain*, the States General of the *United Provinces*, and the United States of *America*, and enjoining the Obſervance thereof.

GEORGE *R.*

HEREAS Proviſional Articles were ſigned at *Paris*, on the Thirtieth Day of *November* laſt, between Our Commiſſioner for treating of Peace with the Commiſſioners of the United States of *America* and the Commiſſioners of the ſaid States, to be inſerted in and to conſtitute the Treaty of Peace propoſed to be concluded between Us and the ſaid United States, when Terms of Peace ſhould be agreed upon between Us and His Moſt Chriſtian Majeſty: And whereas Preliminaries for reſtoring Peace between Us and His Moſt Chriſtian Majeſty were ſigned at *Verſailles* on the Twentieth Day of *January* laſt, by the Miniſters of Us and the Moſt Chriſtian King: And whereas Preliminaries for reſtoring Peace between Us and the King of *Spain* were alſo ſigned at *Verſailles* on the Twentieth Day of *January* laſt, between the Miniſters of Us and the King of *Spain*: And whereas, for putting an End to the Calamity of War as ſoon and as far as may be poſſible, it hath been agreed between Us, His Moſt Chriſtian Majeſty, the King of *Spain*, the States General of the *United Provinces*, and the United States of *America*, as follows; that is to ſay,

That ſuch Veſſels and Effects as ſhould be taken in the *Channel* and in the *North Seas*, after the Space of Twelve Days, to be computed from the Ratification of the ſaid Preliminary Articles, ſhould be reſtored on all Sides; That the Term ſhould be One Month from the *Channel* and the *North Seas* as far as the *Canary Iſlands* incluſively, whether in the Ocean or in the *Mediterranean*; Two Months from the ſaid *Canary Iſlands* as far as the Equinoctial Line or Equator; and laſtly, Five Months in all other Parts of the World, without any Exception, or any other more particular Deſcription of Time or Place.

And whereas the Ratifications of the ſaid Preliminary Articles between Us and the Moſt Chriſtian King, in due Form, were exchanged by the Miniſters of Us and of the Moſt Chriſtian King, on the Third Day of this inſtant *February*; and the Ratifications of the ſaid Preliminary Articles between Us and the King of *Spain* were exchanged between the Miniſters of Us and of the King of *Spain*, on the Ninth Day of this inſtant *February*; from which Days reſpectively the ſeveral Terms above-mentioned, of Twelve Days, of One Month, of Two Months, and of Five Months, are to be computed: And whereas it is Our Royal Will and Pleaſure that the Ceſſation of Hoſtilities between Us and the States General of the *United Provinces*, and the United States of *America*, ſhould be agreeable to the Epochs fixed between Us and the Moſt Chriſtian King:

We have thought fit, by and with the Advice of Our Privy Council, to notify the ſame to all Our loving Subjects; and We do declare, that Our Royal Will and Pleaſure is, and We do hereby ſtrictly charge and command all Our Officers, both at Sea and Land, and all other Our Subjects whatſoever, to forbear all Acts of Hoſtility, either by Sea or Land, againſt His Moſt Chriſtian Majeſty, the King of *Spain*, the States General of the *United Provinces*, and the United States of *America*, their Vaſſals or Subjects, from and after the reſpective Times above-mentioned, and under the Penalty of incurring Our higheſt Diſpleaſure.

Given at Our Court at *Saint James's*, the Fourteenth Day of *February*, in the Twenty-third Year of Our Reign, and in the Year of Our Lord One thouſand ſeven hundred and eighty-three.

God ſave the King.

LONDON:

Printed by CHARLES EYRE and WILLIAM STRAHAN, Printers to the King's moſt Excellent Majeſty. 1783.

Acknowledgements

The authors wish to thank the Director and staff of the National Maritime Museum for their help, particularly the Departments of Ships, Manuscripts and Pictures. They would also like to thank the Musée de la Marine, the Nederlands Historisch Scheepvaartmuseum, the Rijksmuseum and the Smithsonian Institution. The following individuals have been particularly helpful: Bob Hamilton, Baas Kist, Dr. Roger Knight, Dr. Philip K. Lundeberg, Samuel L. Morison, Alan Pearsall, Jan-Pieter Puype, Alan Stimson, David Syrett and Tim Tulenko.

The editor would like to thank David Eldred, graduate of the Royal College of Art, for designing this book. The editor would like to especially thank Samuel L. Morison, the distinguished American naval historian, for allowing us to use some examples from his unique collection of prints and slides for this book, some of which came originally from the collection of his grandfather, Samuel Eliot Morison. The editor would also like to thank Judith Harkison for her assistance in collating some of the illustrations used in this book.

Picture Credits

National Maritime Museum, Greenwich: 6–7, 36–37, 61, 65, 114, 130, 136–37, 148–49, 150–51, 154–55.
US Navy: 10–11, 28–29 (by courtesy of the US Naval Academy Museum, Annapolis, Md.), 30, 51, 81, 86, 93, 98–99, 103, 128–29.
From the Collection of Samuel L. Morison: 9, 12, 18–19, 27, 62–63, 70–71, 82–83, 90–91, 118, 122–23, 127, 146–47, 156.
Bibliothèque Nationale, Paris: 2–3
National Maritime Museum/Robert Hunt Library: 138, 142–43.
The Historical Society of Pennsylvania: 158.
Bison Picture Library: 74–75, 85, 94–95.
Yale University Art Gallery: 134–35.

North Sea

CARRICKFERGUS ★

★ **DOGGER BANK**

★ **FLAMBOROUGH HEA**

Atlantic Ocean

Den Helder

Amsterdam

London

Chatham

Plymouth

Portsmouth

Brussels

Boulogne

NETHERLANDS

AUSTRIAN
NETHERLANDS

USHANT ★ • Brest

• Paris

HO

Quiberon Bay

FRANCE

Toulon

Lisbon •

• Madrid

MINORCA

Cadiz •

GIBRALTAR ★

Mediterranean Se